THE PURPOSED BRIDE

Lindsay Tracy Hall

Published by CreateSpace Independent Publishing Platform.

The Purposed Bride is based off of articles previously printed on the blog The Sweet Christian Bride, www.thesweetchristianbride.com.

The Scripture quotations contained herein are from the New Revised Standard Version Bible, copyright © 1989, by Division of Christian Education of the National Council of the Churches of Christ in the U.S.A. Used by permission. All rights reserved.

Cover design by Andee Flynn.

Cover photo © 2013 by Jaime Lauren Photography. All rights reserved.

All bride entries were submitted for use in *The Purposed Bride* and are used with permission by the various authors: Kelly Alexander, Roshelle Baier, Alexandra Beck, Joy Boyan, Julie Davies, Christina Davis, Alyson Drost, Andee Flynn, Tricia Halsey, Krista Lopata, Shannon Milholland, Emily Perschbacher, Kathy Richardson, Elizabeth Shea, Natalie Sorenson, Amber Sutton, Naomi Swertfeger, and Katherine Wolf. Authors listed as anonymous preferred not to disclose their identity.

ISBN-13: 978-0615768090 (ThreeStrands)

ISBN-10: 0615768091

Printed in the United States of America.

ENDORSEMENTS

"In *The Purposed Bride*, Lindsay Tracy Hall has created a one-of-a-kind resource that is incredibly thorough and spiritually sound. It will encourage and guide you as you plan your once-in-a-lifetime wedding!"

-Mary Gothi, co-founder of The Significant Marriage ®

"In her book, *The Purposed Bride*, Lindsay Tracy Hall covers aspects of preparing for a wedding in a God-glorifying manner. Writing practically, specifically, and knowledgeably, the author makes God the focus of all the wedding preparations, premarital events, and the celebration of the wedding day. It is with great enthusiasm that I recommend *The Purposed Bride* to every bride."

-Myrna Alexander, author of *Behold Your God* and *Woman of Wisdom*

"As a mother to four daughters, I openly wept through many of these chapters—not because I dread the future but because I'm so grateful they will be able through this resource to plan a wedding that honors God and the distinctive way He gifted and designed each one of them. With its emphasis on Christ, *The Purposed Bride* will lead you closer to God's heart as your day also draws closer. It will equip and educate you to craft a wedding worthy of a marriage."

-Shannon Milholland, author of *Jesus and My Orange Juice* and *Pre-Praying*

ACKNOWLEDGEMENTS

Above all, thanks be to God for stirring in me thoughts about weddings, for His patience in teaching me what to say, and for the certainty that He will use this book for good in someone's engagement.

To my encouraging husband, I love you. You always believe in me, even more than I do myself. It is with joy that I write this book for you.

And to my family who supports me through the unknown adventure of writing, thanks for standing by in eager anticipation. In particular, thank you to my mother-in-law for being a great cheerleader and marketer for this book.

Thank you also to Kelly Alexander, Roshelle Baier, Alexandra Beck, Joy Boyan, Julie Davies, Christina Davis, Alyson Drost, Andee Flynn, Tricia Halsey, Krista Lopata, Shannon Milholland, Emily Perschbacher, Kathy Richardson, Elizabeth Shea, Natalie Sorenson, Amber Sutton, Naomi Swertfeger, and Katherine Wolf for sharing a piece of their wedding story with me. And to Drew Allen, Andee Flynn, Christina Davis, and Jaime Lauren Photography for their help in constructing this book. To Chris, Mary T., Danny, Ginger, Nate, Myrna, Shannon, Mary G., and Hannah for their early reads and feedback.

Lastly, to the Millers who let me write in their garage-office every morning... thank you deeply!

CONTENTS

Prelude   7
PART I: Purpose   9
PART II: Planning   13
    Budget   14
    Timeline   17
    Venue   21
    Dress   26
    Bridal Showers   31
    Coordination   35
    Rehearsal Dinner   38
    Ceremony   42
    Vows   48
    Reception   52
PART III: People   57
    Your Fiancé   58
    Your Family   61
    Your Bridal Party   65
    Your Guests   69
    Your Vendors   73
PART IV: Paired   77
    Registry   78
    Pre-Marital Counseling   82
    Wedding Night   87
    Honeymoon   94
    Forever   98
Postlude   103
Appendix   105

PRELUDE

A wise woman taught me that no one just falls into a good relationship with God. Nor does anyone fall into abundant life. Both of those take planning, prayer, and perseverance. Creating a worshipful wedding is no different.

You, my friend, who are purposed by our Almighty Lord, are a bride to be reckoned with. Your marriage holds eternal weight, and your wedding is a catalyst for God to work out some of those eternal measures in the hearts of your guests and vendors.

Your engagement period is one of the greatest adventures of your life! In addition to the eternal weight, you get to piece together the building blocks of your dream wedding to marry the love of your life.

Budget limitations, time constraints, unmet expectations, and clashing voices of influence will all try to steal your joy, but with planning, prayer, and perseverance, you can maintain perspective and delight in this time.

My hope is that this book will nurture your joy, remind you to pray, and coach you in how to plan your wedding with godly purpose.

PRINCIPLE

With all of the research that planning a wedding requires, it can be easy to feel saturated with information. Each section in *The Purposed Bride* includes a key principle to godly wedding planning. If you can absorb no other information, just focus on the principles. They will help guide you purposefully in your planning.

PICTURES

Knowing what has worked for others and what hasn't is invaluable (and entertaining). Real-life stories—brief "snapshots" of a bride's day—are included to help inspire you and caution you. PERFECT PICTURES are captured moments that brides relish as an integral part of their dream wedding day. PROBLEM PICTURES are those unfortunate blunders that brides have learned to laugh about over time. Both PICTURES can help you purposefully plan your own wedding day so that your own wedding "pictures" will be rich and delightful.

PERSONALITY IN PRACTICE

You and your fiancé are unique masterpieces designed by God Himself. The colors of your personalities blend to create a distinct palette. Let that palette set the tone for your wedding because the best weddings always reflect the personalities of the bride and groom.

Your guests will appreciate knowing you better by the color you choose for your shoes, the songs you select for the ceremony, and the ambiance of the venue you book. All the decisions you make point back to what makes you feel like you, so take the information in this book and make it your own. By showing your guests who you are, they will better know who God is, for you were created in His image.

PRAYER

Prayer is your lifeline for every day, and especially for your wedding-planning season. Because prayer connects you to the heart of God yet can be so difficult to prioritize, I have included prayers in every section of this book. Use them, claim them, and incorporate them into your daily planning life. Prayer is always relevant and always worth it.

A blessed and purposed engagement to you!

PURPOSE

"The human mind may devise many plans, but it is the purpose of the Lord that will be established" (Proverbs 19:21).

PRINCIPLE: Believe that God will use you and your wedding for His glory.

God can do mighty things. You've heard stories of His wondrous power before, but let's take it a little closer to home. Imagine you are happily married and living in rural, mid-west America; then, suddenly, a bale of hay is torched by God. As you go to check it out, you hear God's voice tell you to leave where you are and go into the heart of Asia to release persecuted Christians from their abusive governments.

Imagine you are a casualty of an unforgiving economy, and you have nothing in your kitchen but a Cup 'O Noodles and half a package of Saltine crackers. After you eat those, you will have nothing left, so you prepare to eat them with dignity as your last meal. Some man knocks at your door and asks for food and shelter. Although you have nothing substantial to give, your Cup O' Noodles and Saltines feed you both, continuously replenishing themselves as you eat them.

Imagine you are engaged to be married (I know, this one's cheating), and you end up supernaturally pregnant with a V.I.P. in your womb.

These scenarios sound crazy, but they have happened (minus the contemporary adjustments). Scripture is loaded with stories of ordinary people who had extraordinary faith in God's provision and purpose. As you plan your wedding, certainly cross your *t*'s and dot your *i*'s to make sure

9

everything is smooth and spectacular, but don't forget to plan with eternal purpose. It's not about whether the day goes off without a hitch; it's about whether God uses the day to bring glory to His name.

The same God who freed a nation, multiplied a disappearing food supply, and gave the world a savior is the God who loves you, purposed you, and dwells within you. Your wedding could be a miracle that you cannot even begin to fathom! Leave room for God to show up and to make His presence known.

ADVICE FOR WEDDING PURPOSE BLESSINGS

-Be honest about your desires and fears.

-Pray diligently with your fiancé for God to show you His purposes for your wedding.

-Write the purposes down so you have a tangible reference whenever you might need it.

-Communicate your purposes to your family and bridal party, so they can do their best to team up with you in achieving them.

Why are you having the wedding you are having? Why not smaller or bigger? Why not cheaper or more opulent? Why not sooner or later?

For every decision you make, there is a purpose driving it.

PERSONALITY IN PRACTICE

Is the purpose of your wedding to worship God? Is it to honor your family? Is it to throw a great party?

A great exercise to do with your fiancé is to list your wedding purposes. Start individually so you aren't influenced by the other, and then see where your lists complement each other and where they clash. Refine it so you have a core list of purposes that you can both come back to when things get so stressful or tempting or emotional that you need to ask yourself, "Why am I doing this?"

You can also help identify latent purposes in each other that need to be addressed, confessed, and thrown off such as wanting to show off, wanting to spite your parents, or wanting to celebrate yourself. As Jesus says in Mark 7:21, the human heart is where evil intentions come from, so being diligent about searching your heart to identify the selfish purposes will free you up to act on the mighty ones.

Dream big. Pray for God to show you His purpose for your wedding. He used my friend's wedding to turn me back to Him. Maybe He wants to use *your* wedding to do miracles in someone's heart.

PRAYER

Father in Heaven, Your will is perfect. Please show me where my heart is selfish, so that I can confess that as sin. (Confess your sins). Forgive me, Lord, for all of the ways that I have made and will make this wedding and this marriage about myself. What purposes do You have for my wedding, both in this life and in eternity? You know the desires of my heart, You know the limitations of our time and budget, and You know the needs of every person who will be there. Direct my steps and teach my heart to trust Your perfect purpose for this wedding. In Jesus' name, Amen.

PERFECT PICTURE

"Right after Matt proposed he was shipped out overseas again. Because I was planning most of the wedding by myself, I knew that I had to be intentional if I wanted to avoid stress. Matt and I made a list of what was important to each of us and what wasn't. I also made a list of what I wanted on my wedding day, making sure to add in time for prayer throughout the day. Making these kinds of lists and keeping them in my wedding binder where I could see them helped to ground me. We could work backwards from them in order to glorify God with our wedding and to plan a party where Matt and I could really celebrate being husband and wife. It was a source of flooding peace to remember that all we had to do—the only important things for each day—was to honor and adore God, honor each other, and love the people whom God loves. Everything else was just a detail."

-Amber Sutton

PLANNING

"Commit your work to the Lord, and your plans will be established"
(Proverbs 16:3).

There are two practical rules of thumb for wedding planning: 1) have enough time, and 2) have enough money. Simple, right? Let's get started.

BUDGET

"The rich rule over the poor, and the borrower is the slave of the lender"
(Proverbs 22:7).

PRINCIPLE: Spend less than you have.

In biblical times, and even in places today, if someone couldn't pay a debt, they would be "sold" into servitude until the debt was paid. Of course, without their ability to run their farm, or however they made income, that debt would likely continue to accrue.

It sounds like an antiquated idea, but **debt is a form of slavery** today too. Think about the crashing housing market as just one example. People who defaulted were slaves to the banks who dictated whether their homes and other material items would remain their own. Others remained slaves to their mortgages because the economy made their houses too expensive to sell.

Whether it's a defaulted loan, a bounced check, an unpaid credit card balance, or any other sort of unplanned and uncontrolled debt; if we have debt, we will either be slave to the lender or slave to the benefactor who bails us out.

Moral of the story: Don't carry wedding debt into the first year of your marriage.

How much money are you starting with? Does any of that money come with strings attached? Do any of your benefactors have strong opinions about how your wedding should look?

Once you know those answers, you can start working backwards using an online **wedding budget calculator** from any major wedding websites to make sure you are not spending more than you have.

Ask for deals and discounts along the way, and **get creative** with items and connections that you already have. Perhaps you have a service that you can use in exchange for your vendor's service. A perfect wedding doesn't have to break the bank. Keep in mind that God fed 5,000 people from just two fish and five loaves. He can do miracles with your provisions too.

PERSONALITY IN PRACTICE

Spend some time dreaming about your wedding. When you picture where it is, what do you see? Who is there? Who is presiding over your ceremony? What is your bridal party wearing? Is there music in the background? After the ceremony, is everyone dancing? What are people eating? Are you indoors or outdoors? Do you have a traditional wedding cake? Do you leave in a limo?

Have your fiancé dream about his ideal wedding too. After you both have visualized it, write down a list of which aspects are really important to you. Sometimes things come to mind because those are what your heart truly desires. Other times they come to mind merely because of what people have told you or because of weddings you have seen before.

ADVICE FOR BUDGET BLESSINGS

-Pray over the big picture and over every detail.

-Ask for deals, donations, and volunteers.

-Be creative with what you already have.

When you have figured out which aspects of the wedding are truly important to *you*, you can begin to discuss how you will prioritize your budget. Major wedding websites have updated spending averages built into their budget calculators. You can start with these averages and then decide if the percentage of your budget should be higher or lower for each item than the average.

Culinary buffs might want to go all out on the food options; musicians might want to splurge on a band rather than on a DJ; visual people might prioritize flowers and candles. What is important to you may not be important to your fiancé and vice-versa, so having the opportunity to figure out where your differences in priorities lie will allow for a conversation about how to best embrace each other's desires given your financial boundaries.

Be aware that many men will say they don't care what their fiancées choose when, in actuality, they have a strong sense of veto. They often have difficulty creating a vision, but they can easily edit an existing one. If this is the case for your fiancé, be patient with him. You can use your list as a starting point for his responses.

PRAYER

Lord, You are the giver of good gifts. All that we have is Yours. Please use what we already have and bring us what we need in order to honor You with every financial detail of our wedding. Bring favor to us with quality vendors who can offer discounts and deals. With every dollar, be glorified! In Jesus' name, Amen.

PERFECT PICTURE

"Bryan and I did not have a lot of money to spend on our wedding. My parents promised to cover the venue and my dress, but the rest was up to us. We prayed over nearly every decision, and God was so gracious to provide more than we could have dreamed. When I met with the wedding coordinator at our venue, we both made the connection that we had graduated from the same university and that we attended the same church where his wife was a deacon. He offered a significant discount for the venue simply because he wanted to bless Bryan and me. The good news never stopped. Our wedding coordinator volunteered her time for free because she was building her business. She hand-made all the bouquets and centerpieces using wholesale-priced flowers from the LA Flower Mart. Our photographer gave us a deal because I worked in Christian ministry. Our jeweler hand-made necklaces for my bridesmaids and sold them to us nearly at cost, and our friends volunteered to sing during the ceremony. It was obvious that we didn't need to worry. God was working, even in the details."

-Tricia Halsey

TIMELINE

"For everything there is a season, and a time for every matter under heaven"
(Ecclesiastes 3:1).

PRINCIPLE: Schedule time for rest, exercise, relationships, and worship into your wedding-planning timeline.

Living day by day has its pros and cons. The thought of "tomorrow" brings no stress, because it's not yet on the radar; however, there is little preparation for what is to come. Living for a deadline has the opposite pros and cons—you are prepared for what's to come but are too stressed to enjoy the present.

The balance between the two comes from the idea that there truly is **a time for everything**. Creating that balance is a matter of being organized, seeing what is to come, and creating a plan to get there in the designated time frame. Your choices have purpose for the end goal, including when to delegate and when to execute the task yourself. Being organized is for the purpose of peace and thoughtfulness in excellent work.

Some of the most gifted organizers, managers, and planners are the most stressed people. They can envision the end goal and how to get there, but that also means they foresee every hurdle along the way. They tweak every detail until each is perfect, even if the beneficiary of their planning will never even notice. While there is beauty in their intent, there can be stress and sin such as idolatry in their process. Use organization to *remove* anxiety, idolatry, fear, and micromanaging from the picture.

God is an organized God. Look at how He ordered the tribes of Israel or how He designed organisms to thrive in synergy. Perhaps the best example of God's organization is His creation story. He worked for six days, each with a particular goal. When that goal was met, He paused to see that it was good, and then He rested on the seventh day.

We can learn from God how to **backwards map** from our deadline to the present in order to create margins for reflection and rest. As you backwards map, if you find that too many things have to be done in not enough time, that's when you start delegating.

Delegating is an art. You have to find willing, available, trustworthy people who can either take your vision and run with it or follow your instructions at each step without necessarily needing to understand the end goal. Your job is not to micromanage them, but rather to check in with, equip, guide, and release them to do the job entrusted to them.

Your bridal party and family members are your prime pool of "volunteers." Be sure to give them ample direction and advance notice. If they are given the minimum to work with, they will probably give you back a minimal result.

ADVICE FOR TIMELINE BLESSINGS

-Backwards map from the day of your wedding to the present.

-Begin with the assumption that you will not do everything yourself.

-When you delegate, give clear instructions with measureable goals and ample time.

-Honor the Sabbath and daily seek the Lord. That is never a waste of time.

No matter how long your engagement is or whether you have a local or destination wedding, you can find **wedding timelines** galore in major wedding magazines and websites. Find a couple of timelines and piece them together according to your needs. If you work full-time, your timeline will be thinner than someone with full days to plan.

As you match up the suggested timelines with your own calendar, block out certain days or evenings for date nights, time with friends, non-wedding family hang-outs, exercise, and spiritual rejuvenation. You will maximize the time you allow yourself if it's a little, whereas if you are like most people, you will waste the time you allow yourself if it's a lot.

All that to say—if you are minimizing your planning windows for the sake of other good and necessary things, have no fear. Being **balanced in your priorities** reaps reward.

PERSONALITY IN PRACTICE

Fill out this questionnaire using your name or your fiancé's name depending on who better fits the description. Have him do the same (no peaking). Compare your lists and use this discussion to tackle some really big organizational questions such as who will do the research, who will oversee which planning aspects, to whom will you delegate which tasks, how will you check in with each other, who gets to veto what, etc.

Remember to have this conversation with humor and with grace, or save it for a pre-marital counseling session.

1. The more organized person is _____.

2. The clearer communicator is _____.

3. The person with better vision-casting is _____.

4. The better problem-solver is _____.

5. The calmer person is _____.

6. The person who can better communicate with the bride's parents is _____.

7. The person who can better communicate with the groom's parents is _____.

8. The person with more free time between now and the wedding is _____.

9. The more efficient person is _____.

10. The more creative person is _____.

PRAYER

Lord, time is a gift from You. Help us to be prepared, so we use it well. Help us also to plan with an open fist, so we can let go of details that keep us from the joy of the moment. Forgive us for our anxiety, arguments, and disappointments along the way, and teach us how to release all of those to You, the sovereign One who knows all things. Let us fix our eyes on Jesus throughout the planning process. In Jesus' name, Amen.

PERFECT PICTURE

"When planning my Los Angeles wedding while living in Michigan, timing was critical. There was only so much preparation that I could accomplish from out of state, so the time that I spent planning when visiting home had to be organized and purposeful. Coming home for a weekend meant scouting and selecting a venue in two days. Coming home for a week meant selecting all of my vendors and my dress in six days. As an indecisive person, planning a wedding in short but highly focused blocks of time required me to make decisions quickly and definitively. I prepared for my appointments, but beyond that, I had to have confidence that they (the experts) would take my vision and execute it. Once a decision was made, it was time to relax, not to second-guess. I had to be comfortable delegating responsibilities to my mom and to the wedding coordinator (both in Los Angeles) whom I trusted and who were more than happy to help. These planning trips were brief and fast-paced, but once they were over, I was able to focus much more of my time on cultivating my relationship with my husband-to-be, which, ultimately, was the most important preparation of all."

- Alexandra Beck

VENUE

"For which of you intending to build a tower, does not first sit down and estimate the cost, to see whether he has enough to complete it? Otherwise, when he has laid a foundation and is not able to finish, all who see it will begin to ridicule him"
(Luke 14:28-29).

PRINCIPLE: Use your venue as a starting point from which to measure the feasibility of your other wedding details.

Where you choose to have your wedding will shape every other detail. It is the core decision of your wedding planning. You can certainly start your research on other aspects before you have a location pinned down, but to protect your time and wallet, don't put any money down on other things until you have your location secured. You will want to know that your plan is feasible given the context of your venue before you solidify other major details.

Your location will cut out a large portion of your budget upfront. Be sure to also ask about **hidden fees** such as for nicer chairs, colored linens, cake cutting, corkage, overtime, service charges, etc. Sometimes the advertised price is for the basic package, but the advertised pictures boast the expensive package. It's always good to ask about the hidden fees, so you know what your money is buying.

Depending on how many people your facility can hold, your venue will help refine the size of your guest list. Conversely, the **size of your guest list** might narrow down your venue possibilities. Having a basic guest estimate in mind while you are venue shopping is really helpful in saving your time. If you can't fit your guests, move to the next venue.

Another major planning detail influenced by your venue is the **wedding date**. If your prized facility is also every other bride's top choice, then you will lose some flexibility in choosing a date. Come prepared with a couple of dates in mind so that you will know right away if you need to close that door and open another.

You probably have a pretty good vision of what your perfect **wedding dress** looks like, whether you have a veil, and maybe even what jewelry you are donning. If you do, you probably also have a vision of where you will be wearing that dress. In a garden? In a church? On the beach? The picture in your head will help refine your venue search.

ADVICE FOR VENUE BLESSINGS

-Pray for God's guidance and discernment.

-Ask more questions (and write down the answers) than you think you will need to know.

-Consider the people you would be working with at the location. Relationships can make a difference in the quality of your experience.

-Have your top three dates, your estimated number of guests, and your budget figures in mind before venue shopping.

-Weigh a referral more heavily than an advertisement.

If you do not have an idea of your wedding dress, then booking your venue will equip you with context when you go wedding dress shopping. When you look in the mirror, you aren't just evaluating how the dress looks on you, but you are also imagining how the dress will look coming down the aisle of your spectacular venue. It might be a little strange to have a blooming ball gown for a backyard BBQ wedding. You can also plan ahead for whether your ceremony could be subject to wind, heat, cold, snow, or rain, and if so, what kind of veil, sleeves, and shoes would be better than others.

Additionally, consider the **environment** for your fiancé and your bridal party. It's better to keep your beach-bum groomsmen from wearing a tux jacket with their board shorts if you are getting married in a cathedral. Likewise, give your bridesmaids a break by choosing flats instead of heels if you are getting married on a lawn or in the sand.

Food options will be narrowed for you once you determine whether your venue allows off-site catering or requires in-house dining services. From there you can determine buffet versus plated meals, roaming appetizers versus stations, open bar versus cash bar or dry wedding, etc.

Ask your venue contact about their sound restrictions and capabilities. They might already have a **sound system** that you can rent. If not, you will want to determine where their outlets are and where they have previously had success with a band or DJ set-up. If they do offer speakers, amps, and microphones, you can weigh their rental costs against those of your musicians or videographers. Sometimes venues have **sound restrictions** after a certain hour, so be sure to determine those before your heart is set on an all-night, outdoor dance party.

If your venue is a "wedding factory," you have the benefit of relaxing confidently in the hands of people who have done this a million times. You will likely have the downside, however, of being on a tight **wedding-weekend schedule**. Your facility is probably booking a morning wedding and an evening wedding on Saturdays and Sundays. What this means for you is that your morning wedding needs to run on a tight schedule. No time for lingering on the dance floor or eating leisurely if you have a lot of programming. For your evening wedding, you will have limited time on the front end for vendor set-up and for pictures.

If your venue is new to weddings, then you will have the privilege and the responsibility of breaking-in the facility. They will probably be very accommodating to your ideas and time frame, but they might need some extra guidance from you (or preferably from your wedding coordinator) to get from A to B.

Where your venue is geographically will also define many of your other wedding details. How comfortable are you being far away from your venue if you are the primary wedding planner? Are there weather considerations that accompany your wedding destination? How many guests will come if the location is an easy drive away versus needing a plane flight, shuttle, and overnight stay? The closer your venue is to you and your guests, the fewer details need to be coordinated regarding transportation, accommodation, parking, and traffic.

The **geographic location** will also determine which vendors you will be able to use. If you can find ones who have serviced an event at your venue before, or ones who are willing to take a trip out there to ensure no day-of surprises, you have a better chance of vendors working smoothly with each other and with your location.

Ideally, all the set-up and clean-up would be invisible to you. You would just show up and let your **coordinator** do his or her magic. If your venue has a knowledgeable and accessible manager or coordinator, then your vendors can communicate directly with him or her to sort through many logistical details that you don't need to be involved in.

Venue representatives can also show you pictures of how their facility has been decorated in the past. From photographs of prior events, you can glean a sense of how much labor and money you will need to put towards your decorative items. If the location holds enough intrinsic beauty, you might not need to spend as much on **flowers, candles, and other decorations**.

As you can see, determining your venue will point you in the right direction for how much to spend on other things, what to wear, what to eat, when to have the wedding, and a whole host of other factors. If you are planning with purpose, book your venue first because your context for everything else will then become clearer.

PERSONALITY IN PRACTICE

Your location will set a tone for your wedding (even before you decorate it) because of its intrinsic ambiance.

Romantic. Natural. Elegant. Rustic. Intimate. Comfortable. Regal. Modern. Classy. Casual. Homey. Creative. Tropical. Rural. Traditional. Laid-back.

The adjectives you would use to describe your own personality, your own thrive-zone, and the dynamic of your relationship will usually be very similar to the adjectives you would use to create the ideal tone for your wedding.

This exercise is simple, but it will come in handy for helping you and your fiancé to get on the same page regarding what kind of location you want, as well as for determining the tone of invitations, programs, centerpieces, and other details down the road.

Each of you make a list of 10 adjectives that best describe you, 10 adjectives that best describe each other, and 10 adjectives that best describe the dynamic and characteristics of your relationship.

See where your lists overlap. If those adjectives can serve as guidelines for your venue decision, you will both be acting in a way that is *you*. When you can be yourself, the unique masterpiece that God designed, you shine a light on God. No need to force your wedding into a dimly lit ballroom when you much prefer the sunshine and stars of the great outdoors. Be yourself in your wedding planning.

PRAYER

Holy Father, creator of the universe, You are mesmerizing. You are captivating. You are brilliant. All of creation reflects Your beauty, and we want our wedding to reflect that too. Unify our decision about where we should get married. Guide us to venues that let us be ourselves and that would direct people's hearts to You. Use this venue as a tool to orchestrate the rest of the wedding details for Your glory. In Jesus' name, Amen.

PERFECT PICTURE

"My husband proposed on the top of a mountain overlooking the Pacific Ocean. As we exuberantly descended, I pondered building a life with this amazing man in our beloved Los Angeles. But soon pesky logistical questions jarred my reverie. Both of our families were on the East Coast, while we were firmly entrenched with grad school and work in Los Angeles. Where would we get married? Who would plan the wedding? Two options began to crystalize: I could take the reins and assume the gigantic task of independently planning a West Coast wedding, which only a few family members could attend; or I could cede control to our mothers and aunts, who would be over the moon at the chance to plan a hometown wedding to which we could invite hundreds of relatives and friends. Eric and I realized that the details of a ceremony and reception were less important than holding our wedding in a location where all of our loved ones could surround us with love and support. This decision gave us the unique opportunity to relax and enjoy the celebration that our families had so lovingly planned."

-Kathy Richardson

DRESS

"Let us rejoice and exult and give him the glory, for the marriage of the Lamb has come, and his bride has made herself ready; to her it has been granted to be clothed with fine linen, bright and pure" (Revelation 19:7-8).

PRINCIPLE: In choosing a wedding dress that makes you feel like a bride, consider also what reflects you as an ambassador for Christ, a legacy of your family, and a gift to your fiancé.

At a traditional Protestant wedding, guests will be greeted at the door with a program and ushered to their seats. They will wait to the tunes of strings or piano while surveying the flowers along the aisle and considering what the food and reception will be like. Detailed programs might distract them, and of course, any familiar face in the crowd is a welcomed reunion. But what the guests (well, at least most of the female guests) are really waiting for, amidst all the spectacular details they have just observed, is the dress.

What will the bride wear?

The bride's dress is a focal point of the entire wedding celebration. It is an actualized figment of the bride's dreams. There is such anticipation for this singular outfit, and more often than not, it's a vision worth waiting for. The emotional entrance of the bride in all her glory, knowing the fullness of joy that she is about to enter into as she says, "I do"—it is an experience unlike any other.

The truth is, now that I have built up the pressure for you to find the perfect dress, the dress isn't the object of awe. It's you, the bride.

When you find the dress that makes you feel like a bride, you are going to rock that frock down the aisle because of your glow and your presence. You will convey confidence, even if you are nervous. You will have an intentionality and ecstasy that merge to display your beauty to your guests and, of course, to your fiancé.

The dress is just a dress. **It's you in the dress that makes a bride.**

As you dream up your perfect dress and travel from boutique to boutique, you will hone in on what style is appropriate for your venue, what designers are in your price range, and which cuts are flattering on your body.

What you might not consider in the midst of your self-evaluation is **which dress warrants the most pride from the man to whom you will be presented.**

Just as when Jesus returns, His bride will make herself ready to be presented, your bridal preparation—no matter what dress you decide to wear—is a beautiful picture of giving your best to your fiancé who will soon receive you as his beloved wife.

ADVICE FOR DRESS BLESSINGS

-**Pray for discernment.**

-**Ask for deals and discounts.**

-**Stay within your budget.**

-**Avoid bringing too many people dress shopping with you. Having that many opinions can increase your stress level.**

When your fiancé greets you at the altar, are you wearing something that makes him proud to present you at his side? Of course he will think you are beautiful and will be proud to call you his wife, but I mean in the sense of being a crown to his head, as Proverbs 12:4 describes. Does your presence, in person and in attire, make him look better?

Have you asked your fiancé what he envisions when he sees his bride walk down the aisle? Does she have a veil or not? Are her shoulders showing or covered? Is the dress a gown or a sheath?

In addition to being presented to your fiancé, **you are also presented by someone**. For most brides, this is their father. He is handing you over, his precious daughter, and entrusting you to someone else. This is a powerfully emotional event in your father's life.

If you are his pride and joy, does your attire reflect the daughter he is proud of? I don't mean that you have to let your dad pick out your dress. What I do mean is when you let someone into something that is sacred to you—maybe it's inviting a guest into your home or introducing someone to your fiancé—don't you want that person to see what you love about your home or fiancé? It is no different for your father as he gives you away.

Even more importantly, **you are being presented on behalf of your Heavenly Father**. You are a part of the bride for whom Christ will return. And in this earthly life, you are being presented as a testimony of God's work. You are the answer to your fiancé's prayers, and I don't think God takes that lightly. He has been refining you and guiding you so that you will look more like Christ with each day. And God saw it fit for you to be joined as one with this spectacular man whom God has also been refining.

On your wedding day, God presents you to each other as His gift. Your marriage is not an entitlement or anything you deserve; it is a gift from God. When you adorn yourself as the gift from God to your fiancé, you reflect back on God, the giver of good gifts.

What it means for you to wear a dress that pleases your fiancé, your father, and your Lord might be very different from what it means to another bride. For some it means spending little and taking the time and putting in the effort to find a good bargain. For others it might mean donning a more modest gown than your personality warrants. And still for others, it might mean accepting the freedom to find a dress that is 100% you.

PERSONALITY IN PRACTICE

Half the challenge of pleasing someone is finding out what he likes. This simple survey can be given to your fiancé and compared with your own answers (adapt the questions to address yourself) in order to give you some direction as to what type of dress would please your fiancé.

1.   My bride looks most ravishing when

      a.   We go out on dates
      b.   We are just hanging out
      c.   We are playing sports or doing something active

2.   I love it when my bride accentuates her

      a.   Neck
      b.   Shoulders
      c.   Hips

3. When I picture my bride coming down the aisle, she is wearing

    a. A veil over her face
    b. A veil that does not cover her face
    c. No veil; maybe flowers in her hair

4. Concerns I have about my bride's wedding dress are that

    a. My grandmother won't approve
    b. It won't be sexy enough
    c. It will be overdone

5. Financially speaking,

    a. I am concerned about the cost of her dress
    b. Money is no object
    c. As long as she is a good steward of the money, I don't care how much it costs

6. If my bride were to wear an untraditional dress,

    a. I would be fine with it if it makes her happy
    b. I would be fine with it as long as it is similar to a bridal gown
    c. I would be disappointed

PRAYER

Father God, You dress the lilies of the field with splendor, and You give me the very clothes on my back. Help me to be grateful for whatever I wear down the aisle. Show me what would make me glow like a bride while still pleasing You, my fiancé, and my father. Most importantly, let Your Holy Spirit shine inner beauty through me that day. In Jesus' name, Amen.

PERFECT PICTURE

"Finding the perfect dress was high on my list of priorities when it came to my wedding. I didn't really have anything specific in mind, but I knew I was looking for something special and different. I went to one bridal shop with a girlfriend and tried on a few dresses, but nothing blew me away. Then, on a trip back home to Wisconsin, I was visiting my grandma and talking about wedding stuff. I asked to see her wedding photos. I was sure I had seen them before, but now that I was getting married, I was looking at them with new eyes. I took one look at the photos and fell in love with her dress. I started raving about it: It was so sleek, classy, and vintage! One thing led to another and by the time I left, my grandma was overjoyed that her oldest granddaughter would be wearing her dress. I went back to the old farm house where she kept it and opened the cedar chest to find it perfectly preserved. I carefully packed the dress in my suitcase to take back to NYC. There I found an amazing costume designer who used to work on Broadway to make a few alterations. I wanted to keep the integrity of the dress but include a few modern flairs. The first step was adding a burgundy lining to the 8 foot, hand-stitched (by my grandma), peplum, wrap-around train. Then we decided on two decorative appliques for the shoulders, opened up the back of the dress and added all the satin buttons into my bouquet. The dress was finally finished. And on my wedding day, it was so amazing to be walking down the aisle 64 years later in the same dress that my grandma did. The dress I ended up with was beyond perfection; it was priceless!"

-Roshelle Baier

BRIDAL SHOWERS

"Then Moses said, 'I must turn aside and look at this great sight, and see why the bush is not burned up'" (Exodus 3:3).

PRINCIPLE: Use your showers as a time of reflection to stop and marvel at the people God has brought into your life.

It's not every day that we have an opportunity to be surrounded by our beloved friends and family in order to celebrate our lives—birthdays, to a certain extent, and of course funerals, though we won't be alive to experience that.

Weddings are the perfect self-selected reunion. The wedding day itself will probably be too busy or crowded for you to **intimately connect** with all the people you love, but your bridal showers are perfect opportunities to **step aside and look** at the magnificent people God has put into your life. Together with them, you get to take time out of the busyness and simply **celebrate the occasion** of your marriage!

Brides often have a couple of showers that can accommodate people from different life stages or geographies. If you do have **more than one**, you can even have different themes to keep things interesting.

My family shower was an "Around the Clock" theme where people brought a household item off the registry that would be used at whatever hour of the day they were assigned. My sister threw a lingerie shower for me and my girlfriends, which was an entirely different dynamic. And then my mother-in-law flew me up to her home and had a tea-party shower, so I could meet all of her dear friends before the rush of the wedding day.

Some people might ask to host your showers, but you should feel free to ask people to host them if you have someone in mind who would find it an honor to do so. One who would find the invitation a privilege is likely someone who is very close to you. Ask selectively. If you don't know the person well enough for her to say no without putting a strain on the relationship, don't ask.

Similarly, you should also feel free to **express your desires for the shower**, such as wanting less programming and more socializing, or requesting not to play any games that make you feel embarrassed. Sit down with her, and ask her what she has in mind; your hostess won't know your preferences unless you tell her. Expressing your desires within the context of her ideas opens a dialogue and prevents you from appearing as a dictator. Having said that, there will come a point where you have to **release your expectations** into her hands. Hosting a shower is a gift to you, so even if it's not exactly as you would like it, a shower is someone's effort to show you love.

Showers usually involve a time to mingle, refreshments or a meal, a game or program, and the opening of gifts. Favors are usually given to the guests as they leave. Whether you use this traditional format is entirely up to you and your hostesses.

ADVICE FOR BRIDAL SHOWER BLESSINGS

-Clear your schedule that day so your mind won't be racing with your pending errands or appointments.

-Take the time to tell your guests why you are so glad they are there. Blessing others brings joy to the heart.

-Split up clashing groups of people into different showers, so you are not monitoring crowd control instead of celebrating.

Programming is good because it provides a welcomed crutch for people who do not know anyone else at the shower. It's a conversation-starter and a shared experience that can connect people. If the **programming** involves games, it can serve as a great, light-hearted time to let people get comfortable in the environment. If the programming is trivia, it can be an entertaining opportunity for people to get to know you and your fiancé better. Or, my favorite, if the programming is reflective (like a time of affirmations or people making pages in a book to you) then you get to hear how much people love you.

People want to give you gifts, so having a registry, a wedding fund, or a selected charity really helps people to know how to direct their finances for your benefit. It can feel odd asking for a hoard of new items, but people really do want a tangible way to tell you that they support your marriage. As hard as it can be to receive freely, it is a discipline that is necessary if we are to live in community that gives freely.

If you have a strong urge to serve your closest friends and family in the same way that they are serving you at the shower, then by all means, host a brunch or a tea and return the hospitality. When you are at the shower, however, do your best to be present. Use the showers as a true break from your to-do list to relax, to connect, to marvel, to worship, and to simply receive love.

PERSONALITY IN PRACTICE

You might have a shower thrust upon you by an eager friend or family member. If so, accept with grace or tactfully decline. But for the most part, you will have some say in who hosts and in what they plan. To get an idea of what you want, consider the following questions and use them as a starting direction for whom to approach about hosting a bridal shower for you as well as for what elements to suggest.

1) Who among your friends or family members knows you the best?
2) Who among your friends or family members has the time, the resources, and the servant-heart to host or co-host a shower?
3) Whom would you want gathered with you as you celebrate your upcoming marriage?
4) Do you enjoy being in the spotlight?
5) Do you enjoy playing light-hearted games? Trivia games?
6) Would an element of worship be appropriate for the people who are invited?
7) Are there any elements of other showers you have been to that you like or dislike?
8) When are you the most available to take a break and celebrate?
9) Are there particular aspects of your registry that you want your guests to focus on?
10) Are there any themes, food types, music genres, or locations that particularly delight you?

PRAYER

Lord, there is so much to celebrate! Thank You for Your great work in our relationship, and thank You for the dear friends and family whom You have put in my life to love me and to share in my joy. Bless the shower(s) so that it (they) may be a time for me to step aside and marvel at Your presence in my life and in my relationships. In Jesus' name, Amen.

PROBLEM PICTURE

"Our goal was to have a small, intimate wedding. With only 37 of our closest family and friends attending, there was little room for designating a bridal party. It didn't seem like a loss until I looked around and wondered whom to celebrate my bridal shower or bachelorette party with. There were few women to invite—as etiquette dictates only those invited to the wedding should be invited to any other celebration—and even fewer women to consider tapping to host such an event. It came down to a good friend who lives nearby—proximity was key—and a guest list of seven. But two days before the event, two women canceled. My emotions spiraled. I wanted to be celebrated. I wanted to be a priority. I wanted to feel special. But, contrary to society's belief, a wedding season is bigger than 'I.' The shower was canceled with no time to reschedule, and a bachelorette party was never planned, yet I married the man God intended for me, humbled by His plan for our life regardless of the big (party) plans I had for myself."

-Emily Perschbacher

COORDINATION

"Two are better than one, because they have a good reward for their toil"
(Ecclesiastes 4:9).

PRINCIPLE: Make arrangements for a trusted and capable person (or group of people) to relieve you of any duties on your wedding weekend.

The key to enjoying your wedding is to **release all of the details** that you have slaved over into someone else's hands. You don't want to be coordinating the agenda, while getting the gifts in someone's car and making sure that all of the vendors receive their tips—not to mention enjoying yourself. It's too much.

You will want your focus to be on worshipping the Lord, enjoying your husband, and celebrating with your friends and family.

The only way to release yourself from trying to micromanage the day is to hire or arrange for a wedding coordinator, which could be a professional or perhaps a group of extremely reliable friends. If you like to be hands-on in the planning, then just hire a **day-of wedding coordinator**. If you like to be hands-off or if you don't have a ton of time, then hire a **full-scale wedding planner.**

From the moment people gather at your rehearsal to the time you drive away from your reception, someone else should be in charge.

You will want to hire someone competent, affordable, efficient, and trustworthy. One of the other very important qualities in a coordinator is that he or she understands how to **execute tasks in the style of your personality**—or, in other words, that he or she understands what it takes to cast your vision.

During the wedding weekend, a coordinator would work in conjunction with the venue's wedding coordinator if there is one. He or she should have a detailed agenda for the rehearsal, the vendor set-up, the wedding ceremony, the photos/cocktail hour, the reception, and the clean-up. Their agenda should include a minute-by-minute itinerary as well as the names of the people who are in charge of each aspect and their respective phone numbers.

He or she is also the one who makes sure the DJ has the phonetic spellings of all the people in your bridal party. He or she is the one who distributes the envelopes of gratuity to all the vendors. He or she is the one who keeps vendors in line if they are not fulfilling your agreements.

ADVICE FOR COORDINATION BLESSINGS

-Do your research. Whose weddings did you love? Talk to those brides to see if they had an effective coordinator.

-Put everything in writing. A contract will include a general discussion of the job description and your expectations, but also write out in detail all aspects that you are handing over. It will be helpful for your coordinator to have this document for his or her reference when preparing the event.

-Pray in advance that God will help you let go of the details.

PERSONALITY IN PRACTICE

Whom you should hire or ask to coordinate your wedding will be a matter of what kind of control-zone you thrive in.

Are you better at launching and releasing or are you better at following instructions?

Do you have the budget to hire a coordinator or do you have a pool of reliable and available people from which to find a volunteer?

If you had to choose one, would you rather create your dream wedding or be present at your wedding, even if it's not your dream?

PRAYER

Father, please help me find someone who can carry out my visions, to whom I can entrust details, and who would be blessed to be an active part of the wedding. I don't want to miss any moment of my wedding. You know whom I should be asking to coordinate my wedding whether I hire a professional or delegate to trustworthy friends. Show me, and help me to be faithful. In Jesus' name, Amen.

PROBLEM PICTURE

"When my fiancé and I selected our venue, I was pleasantly surprised to find they included an on-site coordinator. She assured me they would take care of set-up and all the details, no help needed. Days before the wedding, she called me asking if her assistant could take over as she was overbooked. I said no problem and asked her to simply review all our previous arrangements with her assistant. After arriving the day of the wedding, I started to go over the agenda with the assistant and she gave me a blank stare. I told her to not worry; my friends (who I was told were unneeded) could help with set up. As I was getting ready upstairs, the assistant handed me the phone. It was the original coordinator who screamed at me, asking where I got off telling her assistant what to do. I tried to apologize and get off the phone as I burst into tears. Just after, my bridesmaids, who know me very well, put their kids on my lap. Someone took a photo of me in that moment, tears streaming down my face and laughing as these two joys brightened my day. I don't remember the picture being taken, but it is one of my favorites. Despite the craziness of the day and the harsh words of the coordinator, God was in control and He reminded me to never forget the joy of a child or what truly matters."

–Naomi Swertfeger

REHEARSAL DINNER

"He said to them, 'I have eagerly desired to eat this Passover with you before I suffer'" (Luke 22:15).

PRINCIPLE: Gather those who are close to you for shared reflection and celebration of the end of one era and the beginning of another.

I love that the last event Jesus planned before His time to be arrested and killed was a meal with His closest companions. It was a time of worship, celebrating the Passover together. It also marked the end of an era. Jesus's death and resurrection would signify the blood of the lamb that was shed for our sins and that covers us from spiritual death. After celebrating Passover with His companions, He became the new Passover Lamb.

The rehearsal dinner also marks the end of an era. It is a truly intimate and nostalgic gathering that closes your time as a single woman. Of course, it also serves as a gathering after a very practical rehearsal—but spiritually and emotionally, it is so much more than that.

A typical rehearsal dinner involves great food and a time of **sharing and toasting**. Traditionally, the rehearsal dinner is hosted by the groom's parents.

One way for the hosts to direct the programming is to invite friends and family members to **share an affirmation or a memory** about the bride or groom or a blessing for their marriage. This is where the great stories come out and where the bride and groom are so deeply warmed and encouraged.

Another way is to give advance notice that guests will be able to take the microphone, literally or figuratively, and invite people to come prepared with **presentations** of some sort. These may be hilarious instructions for how to be married to the other person, skits about how the bride and groom used to be versus who they have become, poems of affirmation, or the like. The scope of the presentations will vary according to the creativity of your guests, but be sure to mention a time limit, so no presentation will monopolize the evening.

To avoid having a lopsided number of presentations, you might consider having a neutral party moderate this portion of the programming. That way, he or she can ask for volunteers from the groom's side if the presentations have all been from the bride's friends, and vice versa.

Both sets of parents can **toast or roast** their children. It's a fun way for them to tell others what they love about you and to tell your fiancé and you what you will need to know about living with the other person—sweet and good humored shout-outs. If you are not on good terms with your parents such that this would be inappropriate, honor them by informing them upfront that there will not be an opportunity for them to take the microphone. Communicating clear expectations with them can go a long way in meeting the needs of their heart during this time.

ADVICE FOR REHEARSAL DINNER BLESSINGS

-Have a plan and keep it as loose as time will allow. Structure is good, but room within that will encourage friends and family to share and present thoughtfully.

-Keep the presentation in between courses or after the meal, so everyone can be present during the celebration.

-If your dinner is at a restaurant, reserve a private room or patio, so you aren't competing with the noise from the restaurant patrons.

-Prepare any statements of thanks or affirmations in advance, so you are not bumbling awkwardly about someone.

The rehearsal dinner is also a perfect place for you and your fiancé to tell your parents and your bridal party how much you love them and are grateful for their support in your wedding and marriage. If you have **gifts or notes for your bridal party**, you can present them and use that as an opportunity to introduce each member to everyone else at the dinner. Telling your bridal party why you handpicked each one of them is a blessing you can freely give.

The same is true for your parents. If you have a **thank you gift or note** for them—not only for their help in putting your wedding together, but also for their presence and support in your life—then you can spotlight them during the rehearsal dinner.

Your friends and family who are celebrating with you this evening will come to know each other so much more by the stories that are told and by the shared experience of the evening. This makes the wedding the next day so much more fun!

PERSONALITY IN PRACTICE

Take some time to jot down who is in your bridal party, why you chose them, and a great memory you have shared with them. Then list your family members, something they have taught you, and your favorite personality trait of theirs. Have fun with this, and as you reflect on each person, thank God for them and pray for them.

PRAYER

Lord God, You are One who gathers. You have brought each one of these people into my life for a time and a reason. Show me how I can bless each one of them, and open my heart to store up the love and encouragement that will transition me from one era to another. In Jesus' name, Amen.

PERFECT PICTURE

"Brandon's mother was a mom of three boys who always longed to have a girl. I knew there was an unspoken desire to help plan more than the rehearsal dinner and, although I realized there might be tension along the way, I felt God was calling me to include my soon-to-be mother-in-law in as much of the wedding plans as possible: picking out the dress, the cake decorator, and the florist, and (because she offered) I let her choose the reception location and plan those details too. She went above and beyond with her time and finances to make our day so special. The rehearsal dinner was held at their country club. It was a night filled with funny and touching stories and music. Brandon and I wanted to make sure his mom felt especially appreciated and loved for her hard work. I wrote her a song and sang it for her in front of our friends and family. 'I'm proud to be the one who stands beside your son, and I see your reflection in the man that he's become. You can rest assured when I say that he'll be in good hands just the way he always has…' She was in tears and to this day boasts of that gift."

-Elizabeth Shea

CEREMONY

"He said to him, 'Bring me a heifer three years old, a female goat three years old, a ram three years old, a turtledove, and a young pigeon.' He brought him all these and cut them in two, laying each half over against the other [...] As the sun was going down, a deep sleep fell upon Abram, and a deep and terrifying darkness descended upon him. [...] When the sun had gone down and it was dark, a smoking fire pot and a flaming torch passed between these pieces. On that day the Lord made a covenant with Abram"
(Genesis 15: 9-10, 12, 17-18a).

PRINCIPLE: Because your marriage is a covenant that echoes God's covenant with His children, your wedding is also a worship ceremony.

Our marriage covenant is an echo of the covenant that God made with us, which is rooted in the one He first made with Abraham—that Abraham would be the father of many nations.

The method of making a covenant involved dividing sacrificial animals into halves and arranging them for the oath. The space in between the halves was a holy space. The two parties would state the terms of agreement including a curse that would apply if the covenant was not upheld. An exchange of property would often be made as a demonstration of consent to the oath.

God made a covenant with Abraham in that way except He brought a deep sleep on Abraham (Genesis 15:12). Instead of Abraham taking part in the sacrifice and vowing to fulfill the covenant, God did all of it. His covenant was fulfilled solely by His own doing, which meant that even if Abraham didn't fulfill his end of the binding agreement, God would. He alone was responsible for fulfilling the covenant. We only see this type of one-sided covenant in the Old Testament with Abraham and with Noah.[1]

God makes other covenants in the Old Testament as well, most notably His covenant with Moses, which demonstrated God's love to the Israelites through the Mosaic Law. Jesus fulfilled this covenant with His death and resurrection (Matthew 5:17) becoming the New Covenant. By the sacrifice of His body and the shedding of His blood, the covenant between God and His children was fulfilled (2 Corinthians 5:21). We can do nothing to earn salvation (Romans 3:28), for Jesus alone fulfilled the terms of the agreement.

A marriage is the same concept, a binding agreement between two people that is made possible because **God fulfills the covenant through us**. Even if one spouse does not fulfill his or her end of the agreement (which is bound to happen now and again), the other is still called to fulfill the covenant 100%. Both parties are to give 100%, not 50/50. God makes this possible.

ADVICE FOR CEREMONY BLESSINGS

-Pray over every detail.

-Give your pastor, your wedding coordinator, and every bridal party/family member a copy of your ceremony outline, so they can facilitate the order of events.

-Record the ceremony. Even if it's done by an amateur videographer, you will want to remember the beauty, the emotion, and the devotion that you had during your wedding.

-Make arrangements for a sound system. People want to hear what's going on, and you won't want them to miss it!

The wedding ceremony is designed to seal this covenant and to draw worship unto the Lord. Many of the ceremony traditions are reminders of the Hebrew covenant ceremony or of the New Covenant such as the aisle representing the holy space between the sacrificial animals, as well as representing the temple veil that was torn. [11]

The rings that are exchanged, the vows that are promised, the communion that is shared, and any sort of unity ceremony that is performed are also symbolic gestures that demonstrate the unity of the marriage covenant.

Scripture readings, songs, the homily, and other recitations are all meant to point people's hearts to the Lord.

In a traditional Protestant wedding ceremony, you will find the following elements:

- Processional of mothers and grandparents
- Entrance of pastor and groom
- Processional of bridal party
- Processional of bride
- Greeting, welcome, and opening prayer
- Introduction of what marriage is and why people are gathered here today
- Presentation of the bride, typically by her father
- Statements of intent when the bride and groom say "I do" in response to marriage commitments. These are the vows made between the bride and the Lord as well as between the husband and the Lord. [III]
- Scripture reading
- Hymn or worship song
- Homily, which is a Scripture-centered teaching about marriage
- Vows, which are the promises made between husband and wife
- Rings, which are an exchange of unity symbols serving as a pledge to be faithful to the covenant
- Communion, unity candle, rose ceremony, or other "first act" as husband and wife
- Pronouncement of husband and wife
- Kiss (oh yeah)
- Presentation of husband and wife
- Recessional

You can **alter the traditional elements to suit your personalities, your time frame, and your audience**. What is most important is that your vows are given to each other and to God before witnesses. All else is a combination of worship and tradition.

PERSONALITY IN PRACTICE

Designing the ceremony is often one of the last planning elements completed, but it's no easy task. If it's possible to borrow an outline from a ceremony you have seen and liked, that would be a helpful starting place. If you are starting from scratch, however, you can look at it in terms of three general purposes: The union of you and your fiancé, the evangelism to non-believers, and the fellowship of believers. All of these are to be for God's glory.

Using those three aspects to help break down the ceremony elements can help you decide whether you want each element or not, and if so, how you want them to be executed. You will then have purpose for each element in your ceremony.

Union of spouses:

- **Statements of intent:** What do you intend to do by being married? How do you intend to do that?
- **Scripture reading:** Which Scripture passages have directed your relationship with God and with each other?
- **Vows:** Do you prefer traditional vows or original vows? Reading, repeating, or reciting?
- **Rings:** What do these rings symbolize to you? What are you pledging by exchanging these?
- **Kiss:** How would you both feel most comfortable kissing in front of everyone?
- **Rose ceremony, unity candle, sand ceremony, lasso:** Which traditions, if any, are special to you? Are there any that you can personalize more than others?
- **Communion:** Do you want to share in the elements together as your first married act of corporate worship? What would your guests be doing while you do that?

Evangelism:

- **Introduction of marriage and ceremony:** How can you explain what a covenant marriage is, so non-believers can hear—maybe for the first time—how God designed marriage?
- **Statements of intent:** How would you explain your purpose and commitment in a Christian marriage in a way that will serve as a model of marriage for non-believers?
- **Scripture reading:** What Scripture passages moved you to first surrender your life to Christ? Which passages speak of God's character?
- **Vows:** How can your promises to each other serve as an example of godly love and marriage?
- **Prayer:** Would your prayer invite non-believers to draw near to the heart of God?

Fellowship:
- **Scripture readings:** What Scripture passages can be an encouragement to married believers among your guests?
- **Prayer:** What thanksgiving, adoration, supplication, or confession do you want to express together with your brothers and sisters in Christ?
- **Communion:** If you offer communion, do you open it up to any believer or do you keep it for just the two of you?
- **Worship songs:** What songs will draw your hearts together in worship and celebration?
- **Vows:** Will you also ask your guests to vow to support your marriage? To renew their own vows as they hear yours?

PRAYER

Father, I know at the end of the day, I will be married, and that is so exciting! Show me how to plan a ceremony that is special for us but that would also show Your love and truth to those who don't know You, as well as to those who do. Let the covenant of our marriage point people towards the New Covenant in Christ Jesus. Fill our wedding with worship. In Jesus' name, Amen.

PROBLEM PICTURE

"I had dreamt of having the perfect wedding day, but most importantly Marc and I wanted our ceremony to be Christ-centered and reflect our personalities and hearts for Jesus. We wanted every detail to be glorifying to Him. Many moments before and after the ceremony, however, were not glorifying to God. I was trying to make this day as holy as possible, but things started to go wrong. Despite the disasters, God did a miracle and completely surrounded and protected our ceremony. As soon as the doors opened and I walked down the aisle to 'How Beautiful' by Twila Paris, my focus was redirected back to the Lord and to the man I was about to marry. The ceremony was perfect—more than I dreamed it would be. This was constantly being confirmed when guests came up to us months later telling us it was the most Christ-centered wedding they had ever attended. If the problems beforehand had not been so difficult, I might not have recognized the Holy Spirit's presence during our ceremony. We wanted the ceremony to draw people into the presence of the Lord as they witnessed us taking our vows before our Almighty Father in Heaven, and with God's help, we were able to accomplish that."

-Julie Davies

[1] *Works consulted for accuracy of information are*
Delbert R . R. Hiller. Covenant: The History of a Biblical Idea. Baltimore: Johns Hopkins, 1969. p 103.
Fairchild, Mary. "Christian Wedding Traditions and Customs: Understanding the Biblical Significance of Wedding Traditions and Customs." About.com. Web. 24 June 2011.

[II] *Works consulted for accuracy of information are*
Child, Brevard S. Introduction to the Old Testament as Scripture. Philadelphia: Fortress Press, 1979
Fairchild, Mary. "Christian Wedding Traditions and Customs: Understanding the Biblical Significance of Wedding Traditions and Customs." About.com. Web. 24 June 2011.
Pettigrew, Larry D. "The New Covenant." The Masters Seminary Journal. 10.2 (1999) 251-270. Accessed via Expositor.org http://www.expositor.org/tmsj/1999/tmsj10q.pdf. 05 October 2012.

[III] *I was introduced to this concept of saying vows to God in the statements of intent by Tim Keller in his book The Meaning of Marriage.*

VOWS

"Whatever your lips utter you must diligently perform, just as you have freely vowed to the Lord your God with your own mouth" (Deuteronomy 23:23).

PRINCIPLE: Know what you are promising when you enter into a covenant marriage because you are vowing before God.

The vows are such an essential part of the wedding ceremony that they deserve their own section in this book. By the power vested in the governmental figure presiding over your ceremony, your marriage contract and your pastor's declaration is what legally binds you in marriage.

God desires for us to respect our laws and legal authority, so the legal aspects of marriage are still important and good. The power vested in the Holy Spirit, however, gives credence to a different determination of marriage. In God's eyes, it is the vow that husband and wife make (and of course the union of sex) that determines a man and woman to be husband and wife. The vows are the **covenant**, whereas the marriage license is only proof of a contract.

Your **vows are holy**, and they are intended for the duration of your life. Pray through them and spend time on them, so you are not rashly or emotionally promising things that you do not intend to keep.

Vows are fulfilled only in an outflow of one's pursuit of Christ. The only things we can commit to for the duration of our lives are those that are rooted in the Lord, for even if we fail along the way, our desire for Him will always keep us moving in the direction of holiness. Most vows take biblical root in Ephesians 5:28-29 and Exodus 21:10 with a promise to cherish each other, as well as to provide food, clothing, and conjugal rights to one another (or to care for and honor each other). [1]

If you are writing **original vows**, one of the easiest formulas is to 1) tell your fiancé what you love about him, and 2) tell him what it means for you to be his wife.

The first part creates a personalized context for the second, which is your promise to him. As you tell him what it means to you to be his wife, you are defining the woman you are committing to become because of your love for him and for the Lord.

You might instead choose to use **traditional vows** or **adapt a passage of Scripture** into vows. This option is great too. There is something utterly romantic about joining the legacy of Christian marriages before you by cherishing the same vows that other brothers and sisters in Christ have faithfully lived out.

ADVICE FOR VOW BLESSINGS

-**Root your vows in God's Word.** Center them around His design for marriage.

-**Have your vows completed at least a month before your wedding.** Vows often get lost in the last-minute jumble of wedding details, yet they deserve to be prioritized.

-**Pray that God will bring you either traditional vows that will speak to your marriage or original words that are uniquely created for your marriage journey.**

Logistically speaking, if you are not used to public speaking and memorization, avoid the pressure of **reciting your vows** from memory. Your pastor can keep a copy of your vows that he or she can prompt you from as you **repeat your promises,** or he or she can give you the copy at the appropriate time so that you can **read your vows**. If you do decide to memorize and recite your vows, make sure your pastor has a copy of them in case you get stuck on a certain line.

Additionally, **arrange for a sound system**. Your vows are the most intimate, personalized, significant part of the ceremony, and your guests who are sitting in the back want to hear what you say to each other. Often there will be a microphone that the pastor is using, which you can step up to. Or, if you are using a videographer, the groom will likely wear a lapel microphone that you can scoot in close to.

As you share your vows in front of your guests, you might be demonstrating Christ's love between a husband and wife for the first time to someone. How awesome a testimony is that!

PERSONALITY IN PRACTICE

For Part I of your vows—what you love about your fiancé—answer these questions to get your wheels turning. Before copying and pasting into your wedding cue card, consider what information should be preserved as private rather than as declared before your guests. Also, consider what wording you could use that would communicate to your fiancé that you are thinking in his love language (the mode in which he receives love). [II]

1) What do you love about your fiancé?
2) What sets him apart from any other man that you have cared about?
3) What philosophies, dreams, or moments do you uniquely share?
4) How has he made you a better woman?
5) What excites you about being *his* wife?

For Part II, the vows, think about God's design for marriage and about His purpose for your life. What end goal are you willing to sacrifice for and commit to? Your promises are part of a covenant, so do not make your promises lightly. Make only those that are worth a lifetime of effort to fulfill. When you make them with Christ in mind, they will be.

Also, consider what marriage means to your fiancé. Identify what having a wife means to him so that your promises communicate to him that you are coming alongside *him* as his helpmate, lover, and friend, and not just alongside anyone.

1) What does marriage mean to your fiancé?
2) What hopes does he have for his wife, primarily in terms of her developing character but also in terms of her roles and behaviors?
3) What does marriage mean to you?
4) What is God's design for you as a wife?
5) How would you describe the woman that you want to be? How do you become her within the context of marriage?

Once you and your fiancé have completed these questions and have drafted your vows, consider sending them to trusted married friends (one male and one female) to have an independent eye give you feedback. Especially if your vows are a surprise to each other, having a third party weigh in can help smooth out discrepancies of length, tone, or focus so that your vows to each other are balanced and complementary.

PRAYER

Father, You are the source of all my strength. I can only commit to what I can do in Your name. Give me the words for my wedding vows that would speak intimacy into my fiancé's heart and that would create the template You know I will need in order to be a faithful wife every day. In Jesus' name, Amen.

PERFECT PICTURE

"Vows are the most important part of a wedding. For my (then) fiancé and I, they were a public testimony of our commitment to Christ and to each other. We both knew that the most powerful words could not come from us, but from God alone. Then, a friend encouraged me to take a look at Colossians 3:12-17. After just one reading of this passage, we knew without any doubt that these words were exactly what we wanted to promise each other in front of everyone we loved. We spent a date night sitting over my kitchen table, in tears, editing the passage as though we were saying it to each other. When we read the vows to our pastor, she said they were the most beautiful she'd ever heard. When we said them to each other on our wedding day, we meant every word. We still have them hanging on our wall on hand-written note cards seven years later."

-Anonymous

[I] Instone-Brewer, David. <u>Divorce and Remarriage in the Church: Biblical Solutions for Pastoral Realities</u>. Downers Grove: InterVarsity Press, 2003. p 128-129.

[II] *The term "love language" is borrowed from the following book*
Chapman, Gary. <u>The 5 Love Languages: The Secret to Love That Lasts</u>. Chicago: Northfield Publishing, 2010

RECEPTION

"I will bless the Lord at all times; his praise shall continually be in my mouth. My soul makes its boast in the Lord; let the humble hear and be glad. O magnify the Lord with me, and let us exalt his name together" (Psalm 34:1-3).

PRINCIPLE: Consider your reception as an extension of the worship in your wedding ceremony rather than merely as a party.

The purpose of a wedding reception is to **celebrate your marriage** with the people you love and who love you. This, of course, would be remiss without gratitude in your heart and on your lips for what God has done for you.

The celebration is unto Him! This doesn't mean that you have to have a church service at your reception, but it does mean that the celebration is an **extension of the worship ceremony** you just had. The dancing, the eating, the toasting, the programming, the mingling, the laughter, the jubilation...they are all good gifts from the Lord.

How do you want to magnify the Lord with your guests? What brings you most joy? What is your language of thanksgiving? How can you serve your guests with Christ's love as you celebrate your marriage with them?

Traditionally, a wedding reception includes the following:
- The presentation of the bridal party
- The presentation of the bride and groom
- The bride and groom's first dance
- The father-daughter and mother-son dance
- A welcome by the host
- A blessing of the food
- Refreshments or a meal
- Toasts
- Dancing
- Bouquet toss
- Garter toss
- Cake cutting
- Send-off

What you choose to do is up to you and your fiancé. When you are most comfortable and having fun, your guests will follow suit. If any of the **traditional reception elements** cause you stress that steals your joy, take that element out. If you want to add something that will enhance the celebration, like a slide show, a money-dance, or a song to your honey, add it in.

> **ADVICE FOR RECEPTION BLESSINGS**
>
> -Make a list of "play" and "do not play" songs for your **DJ**.
>
> -If you are having dancing, get your guests on the dance floor before they sit to eat; they will be more likely to return to the dance floor later.
>
> -Remember to eat.
>
> -Greet your guests or have a sweetheart table where they can approach to greet you.

As your heart is loving the Lord and celebrating with others, you will be inviting others into worship to magnify the Lord with you.

PERSONALITY IN PRACTICE

What is your worship language? [1] Use that to direct your reception elements. If you are worshiping throughout the party, then others will be drawn to celebrate with a worshipful heart too.

Song: If singing to the Lord is your primary worship language, consider adding some worship music into your background music repertoire, sing a song to your husband, give CDs as your guest favors, use song titles/lyrics as your table names, or select a song to dance to with your husband that tells a story.

Dance: If dancing draws you into worship, then you are set. Make sure to save time to actually get on the dance floor.

Scripture: If reading the written Word is what focuses your eyes on the Living Word, then find ways to incorporate that into the evening. Keep your favorite verses by your plate so you can glance at them, put verses on each person's name card, include Scripture in your slide show, recite a section of Scripture to your husband, or introduce your bridal party with a Scripture verse that represents them.

Nature: If being in God's creation brings you into worship, then have your reception outdoors or at a restaurant that overlooks the ocean. Use flowers and plants as your main décor. You can even use mini tree stumps with a groove carved in them as name card holders or give flower seeds as your guests' favors.

Fellowship: If being together with other believers heightens your heart for worship, then put your most beloved friends at your table. Make sure you get to have meaningful conversations during the evening, and not just quick greetings. Dance with each other and break bread together with a corporate heart for the Lord.

Prayer: If prayer is your worship language, then you are lucky. You can practice the presence of God by praying throughout all that you do. But if more guided prayer is helpful, then make sure there is corporate prayer before the meal and perhaps in other portions of the reception. Ask others to be praying for you. You might even pull a girlfriend or your husband aside and take a quick prayer break before returning to the dance floor.

PRAYER

Holy Father, You are the source of all joy and of every good gift. The celebration for our marriage is all for You and through You. Show us how to make our wedding reception an extension of worship that would ignite other believers' faiths and that would show non-believers how truly fun, good, and spectacular You are. In Jesus' name, Amen.

PERFECT PICTURE

"Romance, beauty, adventure—I wanted it all at the reception! We wanted our wedding reception to represent some of our most romantic times together. One of the things we were fortunate enough to do while dating and engaged was to visit some beautiful vineyards and wineries. So for our wedding reception, we picked a property that would mirror the rolling hills of a vineyard; and on the patio before dinner, we had a late afternoon of wine tasting and featured wines from the vineyards we had traveled to together! As the sun set, we moved into the dinner area and enjoyed our wedding feast with homemade sangria and port from Portugal! We also felt that a wedding should have a beautiful, detailed menu. So we made sure to frost the grapes and to have aged cheese, bowls of chunks of chocolate and a cake for each table. We felt having these details at the reception would be a way to invite our guests to share in some of our most romantic adventures and, at the same time, let them know how grateful we were to them for celebrating with us."

-Natalie Sorenson

[1] For information on how to determine your language of worship, read
Thomas, Gary. The Sacred Pathways: Discover Your Soul's Path to God. Grand Rapids: Zondervan, 2010

PEOPLE

"I give you a new commandment, that you love one another. Just as I have loved you, you also should love one another. By this everyone will know that you are my disciples, if you have love for one another" (John 13:34-35).

Your wedding will put you continuously face to face with a number of people whom you may or may not want to love. As a bride for Christ, you have a charge to love them humbly and impartially. Let's talk about how to do this.

YOUR FIANCÉ

"…I found the one whom my heart loves" (Song of Solomon 3:4a).

PRINCIPLE: Your engagement is a time of moving towards oneness.

Of every man you have encountered, your fiancé is the one you have chosen to be **set apart** as yours, and you as his. To choose to faithfully join lives with this man must mean that you have found the one whom your heart loves.

I love the passage in Song of Solomon that reads, "Many waters cannot quench love, neither can floods drown it. If one offered for love all the wealth of one's house, it would be utterly scorned"(8:7).

Love endures through its natural opposition, through tragedy, and through our own depravity. Love cannot be purchased; it cannot be conjured or feigned.

When you love, you have truly received a miraculous and holy gift from the Lord that is backed by His strength and worth.

For the duration of your or his life, you will be charged with making your husband look more like Jesus—in other words, doing all that you can do to spur him on to holiness and to companionship with God. As you move towards **oneness** in your engagement, this charge will begin to take root. You are preparing your life to transform into one with his.

What this means for your wedding planning is that your eyes need to be on the prize. You are marrying *him*. Your wedding is because of your marriage, not the other way around.

No matter how busy you are, how stressed you feel, or how excited you become, your fiancé needs to come before your wedding. Love him by prioritizing him.

One of the most fun ways to prioritize him is to block off time (in advance) to **have date nights**. Just you and him, perhaps your favorite restaurant or a new excursion, but no wedding talk. Enjoy each other outside of the context of wedding planning. Remind each other that you enjoy *being* with each other. This keeps the connection fresh and the priorities ordered.

Another way to prioritize him—a very important one—is to **listen** to his opinions, his fears, his excitement, and even his everyday rambles. If he is shutting down in the face of wedding planning, discern whether to draw him out with questions or whether to let the topic rest. If you have trouble remembering what he says, write it down. Put his thoughts into practice, so he can see from your actions that you have heard him, considered him, and acted for his benefit.

> **ADVICE FOR BLESSINGS ON YOUR FIANCÉ**
>
> -Pray for him always.
>
> -Ask him how he is doing.
>
> -Keep a journal of what you admire about him on that particular day.
>
> -Remember that serving your fiancé is also serving your team. Humility is a blessing for both of you.

Be sure to **pray for your fiancé** and to **pray with him**. He might never know the words that pass from your heart to God's ear, but God certainly does. He is a God who hears and responds! Praying for and with your fiancé will test your faith, your patience, and your hope, but there is nothing that can top the power of prayer spoken out of a heart of love to a God of love.

If you are intentionally scheduling in relationship time (and health time, quiet time, etc.) to your wedding-planning season, you might find yourself relying on routine to establish and protect these good patterns. If your routine starts to feel like a rut, spice it up. **Serve and surprise your fiancé**. Take a regularly scheduled date night and make it all about him. Pick him up and take him to his favorite restaurant. Treat him to a sporting event or his favorite movie. Or stay in and wash his feet, read him a love letter, give him a present, or invite his buddies to join you for a game of poker. Any way that you can speak to his love language, especially outside of the normal routine, will communicate a big, fat, "I LOVE YOU."

PERSONALITY IN PRACTICE

What is your fiancé's love language? [1] If you don't know, ask him. Then make a list of 10-20 different things you can do to speak love to him.

Now the fun part: Go do them!

PRAYER

Lord, thank You for blessing me with the most amazing man in the whole world! I know I don't deserve him, so I want to cherish him every moment. Help me to prioritize him above the wedding. Give me words or actions that I can offer him as a demonstration of my love, all for Your glory. In Jesus' name, Amen.

PERFECT PICTURE

"Avery and I spent nearly all of our dating and engaged relationship hundreds of miles apart. The long distance relationship was tough at times, but it challenged both of us to think of creative ways to show each other our affection. We began writing notes by hand that we mailed at least once a month. Although we talked constantly on the phone and via Skype, the letters were a very sweet way for us to express how we were feeling. It was such a joy to come home from school or work and be blessed by a thoughtful letter from my fiancé. We continued writing letters through our engagement, which was a great way to take a break from wedding planning and refocus our attention on just us. The last letter we wrote to each other was on our wedding day. Avery's letter to me was addressed to "My Bride," and it is a treasure that I will cherish forever."

-Alyson Drost

[1] *The term "love language" is again borrowed from Gary Chapman's book The 5 Love Languages. To identify your love language, take the quiz at http://www.5lovelanguages.com/profile*

YOUR FAMILY

"…but as for me and my household, we will serve the Lord" (Joshua 24:15b).

PRINCIPLE: You can't choose your family and you can't change them, but you can choose to love them and pray for God to change them.

You don't get to choose who your family is. Your parents or siblings or extended family could be toxic or they could be life-giving. Either way, you have a choice how you respond and initiate. It might be an excruciating choice, but it is a choice nonetheless. You can act in the hope that one day, even if not in your lifetime, your family will be one for the Lord.

Even if your relationship with each family member is rooted in vibrant love, you will still encounter difficulties. The reason is trifold:

1) In becoming someone's wife and figuring out what kind of wife you want to be, you will inevitably be reflecting on **why you are the way you are**, which can create a critical eye.
2) The nature of planning a significant event means frequent opportunities for **miscommunication** between people's conflicting expectations and working under the **stress** of a budget and a deadline.
3) No matter how much they love your fiancé, **your family is experiencing a loss** as you experience a gain.

And, the truth is, the underlying fourth reason is that the enemy will always try to pervert a good thing.

What this means for you is that your wedding-planning time will probably be rife with tender moments that God is using to activate certain realizations in you, as well as with confrontational moments that God is using to change a behavior in you. Change is not easy and it usually comes as a response to trial, but it can lead to healing, freedom, and unity.

Expect conflict. This way you can guard yourself with a prayerful heart, intentional words, graceful ears, and humble actions. When someone else's junk scathes you, you will be prepared to fix your eyes on Jesus and to let Him work redemption through it.

If it's your junk that comes up, take it to the foot of the cross immediately. Process it in pre-marital counseling, petition God for guidance, communicate with necessary parties about it, and offer forgiveness even if it doesn't seem warranted.

Take caution, however, that expecting conflict as a means of preparedness of your spirit is a mere attitude away from embracing cynicism. The intent is to be alert to potential conflicts, not to assume the worst in the members of your family. Do your utmost to **assume the best** in each individual and to **celebrate** with those who love you and have rejoiced when you rejoiced and have wept when you wept. God can help you navigate this tricky balance.

> ### ADVICE FOR BLESSINGS ON YOUR FAMILY
>
> -**Pray over each family member by name.**
>
> -**Listen to their advice.**
>
> -**Spend time with your family that is not wedding related.**
>
> -**Consider including elements in your wedding that they loved about theirs.**

In terms of **incorporating your family into your planning** process or into the wedding itself, that is for you and God to determine. Families that are truly toxic or dangerous might need total separation during this time. With other family dynamics, you might need to yield on matters you want to control. Or maybe you are to stand on your conviction and communicate to your family that their way will not be the one on a particular issue.

Only God knows your particular situation. **The Holy Spirit can guide you** perfectly. No matter in which direction He guides you, however, you are still commanded to **honor your parents** and to love one another. What that looks like is between you and the Lord.

Consider these common **family dynamics** mindfully and prayerfully:

- Siblings who feel rejected or neglected
- The mother of the groom who grieves a major loss as her son will never again look to her as the woman in his life
- The father of the bride who struggles with the emotions of getting older and of competing with the groom
- The parents of the groom who feel left out of the process
- Unmarried siblings who feel jealous
- Children who feel forced to accept a new father
- Step-parents who do not feel honored
- Grandparents who feel left out and under-valued
- The parents of the bride who worry about whether they or their dollars are what makes them significant to their daughter

Hopefully, any trials that emerge will result in healing and reconciliation. Families in the throngs of wedding planning often experience **refining**. But it's not all troublesome! In the midst of the trials will also be the sweet, irreplaceable experiences of love and celebration.

PERSONALITY IN PRACTICE

Who are the members of your family? In this particular season of their lives, what major goal, stress, or joy is at the forefront of their minds (aside from your wedding)?

What system of communication does your family practice? Can you schedule times with your family specifically for the purpose of communicating wedding details as well as other times specifically with the restriction of having no wedding talk?

Are there roles in your wedding that play to your family members' strengths?

Have you set aside time to really get to know your fiancé's family?

Which relationship are you most nervous about during your wedding season?

PRAYER

Lord, as You knit me together in my mother's womb, You placed me intentionally in a family. Those around me are no accident. Lord, I confess to You all of the fears I have in dealing with my family during this wedding (confess fears). Please prepare a way for healing, for good communication, for hope, and for celebration. Let me appreciate and encourage them. Above all, let my family be one that lives for You. In Jesus' name, Amen.

PERFECT PICTURE

"When I met my husband, I was already the mother of two daughters. The night he asked me to marry him was also the night he asked them to be his daughters. Our wedding wasn't just a marriage; it was the formation of a family. To mark this, not only did my husband and I exchange vows but he and my daughters did as well. He pledged to care for and protect them as they determined to love and respect him. Choosing a family ceremony set the tone for creating a God-honoring blended family."

-Shannon Milholland

YOUR BRIDAL PARTY

"Some friends play at friendship but a true friend sticks closer than one's nearest kin" (Proverbs 18:24).

PRINCIPLE: Take the time to honor and affirm your friends.

Your friends are treasure. The very fact that they have said *yes* to being in your bridal party demonstrates that they are committed to helping you, to supporting you, and to sharing life with you.

This is such an opportunity to **thank them** for how they have shaped you into the woman you are. Traditionally, you can offer your bridesmaids gifts for being a part of your wedding. Aside from presents, however, there are so many other ways that you can **honor your bridesmaids.**

When you ask them to be a bridesmaid, you can spend some time with each girl, telling her why you are so grateful for her friendship. Or if she lives far away, you can write her a snail mail letter spelling out why you hand-picked her.

At your rehearsal dinner, or as you announce your bridal party at your wedding reception, you can tell your guests who each girl is and why you chose her to stand by your side at your wedding.

You can **incorporate their strengths into your** wedding planning. Assuming that they are available to help with your wedding planning, you can ask your artistic bridesmaid to design your programs, your baker friend to whip up some cupcakes for your cocktail hour, your photographer friend to capture an engagement photo session, and so forth. If they have the capacity to help out, they will likely be honored that you sought out their expertise and entrusted them with wedding responsibilities. If they do not have the capacity to help out, they might feel obligated to say yes because they want to be helpful, so take care to be sensitive and discerning as you approach each person.

The night before your wedding, you can **gather with your bridesmaids** and spend some time relishing the end of your single era.

Maybe you can get your nails done together or join in intimate prayer with one another.

As you seek to honor and thank your friends, keep your eyes open for sensitive spots in your relationships. Weddings can be hard on close friends because they can feel pushed out of your life. For some women, they desperately want to be married and have trouble putting aside their hurt to feel happy for you. Or they might have other circumstances weighing on them that they try to spare you from, but the result is that they are a little more distant than you would like.

Keep your communication lines with them open, both about wedding details and about them. They were your friends before your wedding and will be after, so take care not to let your wedding trump your care for them.

> **ADVICE FOR BLESSINGS ON YOUR BRIDAL PARTY**
>
> -Pray for each member of your bridal party by name.
>
> -Ask them how they want to contribute to the planning or whether they have limitations in helping. No need to be a mind-reader or a dictator.
>
> -Spend time with your bridesmaids apart from the wedding. Ask about their lives too.

In the extreme situation where you must let a bridesmaid go because her behavior is toxic, you should have a conversation with her in private that respectfully outlines her offense and that offers an opportunity for correction. Be clear, but gentle, in expressing to her the consequences if she does not correct her behavior. Know that you are sparing her from making a commitment to you before God that she cannot keep. Even in your anger, love her. Do be aware that you will have a responsibility (for the sake of maintaining a healthy mind and spirit) to process this loss and grieve through it even as you are planning such a joyful event.

PERSONALITY IN PRACTICE

Draw a timeline of the memorable or transformative events in your life. As you reflect on them, write the names of your bridesmaids who shared those experiences with you and walked you through them.

As their names crop up, write down qualities about them that have taught you and shaped you.

Look for opportunities to share these reflections with your bridesmaids, simply to bless them.

PRAYER

Lord, You have blessed me with truly incredible women at my side. Thank You! Each one has shown me a different aspect of Your love. Flood my heart with grace and gratitude so that I may deeply bless each bridesmaid, and show me how I can convey to each one how truly cherished she is. Help me to approach them with listening ears and a humble heart. Give favor to them, Lord, and continue to strengthen our friendships even in the transition from single to married. In Jesus' name, Amen.

PERFECT PICTURE

"The night before my wedding, I gathered all of my bridesmaids into my hotel room so that we could spend some time together talking and praying before we all went to bed. I used the opportunity of this special moment to share a gift with my bridesmaids that was very important to me. Just three months earlier, my mentor passed away, and I wanted to find a way to honor and remember him in my wedding. The way that I decided was best was to give all of my bridesmaids a pearl necklace. My mentor had a ministry to young women, and he wrote a book about this ministry entitled *The Price of a Pearl.* The symbol of a pearl is one of God's transformational power and love that uses uncomfortable and difficult circumstances to craft all of us into His image, into beautiful pearls that reflect His love. The time was a good opportunity to speak truth to my closest friends. It really blessed me to share the truths in which my Heavenly Father clothed me as a single woman, the same truths that my husband now wraps around me as a bride."

-Krista Lopata

YOUR GUESTS

"Now when Jesus heard this, he withdrew from there in a boat to a deserted place by himself. But when the crowd heard it, they followed him on foot from the towns. When he went ashore, he saw a great crowd; and he had compassion for them and cured their sick" (Matthew 14:13-14).

PRINCIPLE: Plan with your guests' welfare in mind in order to show them Christ's love.

The gathering of people you love and who love you is a rare and wondrous occasion! As you walk down the aisle and see the awe on faces of those you are close to and others whom you haven't seen in ages, you will likely be overcome by the reality that they are rooting for you.

How you came to this grouping of people might not have been the perfect picture of peace and joy, but those who were chosen were invited, and here they are at your wedding.

You will be delighted to connect with many different guests at your wedding, while with others it might feel like more of a chore to greet them. Regardless, you are their hostess, their occasion, and their servant.

Servant? Yes, servant.

Jesus served to show love, and He is the prime example for how we are to love. When He and His disciples were exhausted from extensive ministry, they left to find time alone to recharge. When they arrived to their place of retreat, however, the people had managed to show up there.

What probably would have evoked irritation, resentment, and selfishness in any of us in that situation evoked compassion in Jesus. The time of retreat was rightfully His to protect, but He instead served with compassion those who had come to be with Him. He was their occasion.

Your wedding celebrates you, which means you have a right to enjoy it and to take in the honor bestowed upon you by your guests. But if you can receive that honor in order to give it back to those who have gathered around you for this occasion, you will reach deep places in your guests' hearts by your humble, servant love.

A simple way to serve your guests is to connect with them. Thank them for coming, ask how they are, dance with them... Take the time to **greet your guests**, so they will know that their presence was noticed and appreciated.

Another way you can serve your guests is to plan with them in mind. **Put yourself in their shoes**. Will they be sitting in direct sunlight during your ceremony? Will there be any guests who can't eat due to food allergies? Will the music be too loud? Will their heels sink into the grass? Will traffic be horrific as they drive from the ceremony to the reception?

Many of these issues can be addressed in advance. As you consider what you would like and how you would feel with each decision you make, you can reverse the equation and think about what your guests would like and how they would feel. Simply put, the more enjoyable you make it for your guests, the more they will enjoy themselves.

ADVICE FOR BLESSINGS ON YOUR GUESTS

-Pray for each guest by name.

-Make sure the basics of food, drink, and shelter are readily available.

-Consider what you loved or disliked at weddings that you have attended. Apply those considerations to your own wedding.

Jesus says in the parable of the sheep and the goats, "Truly I tell you, just as you did it [gave food, drink, clothing, and visitation] to one of the least of these who are members of my family, you did it to me" (Matthew 25:40). There is incredible glory to God when we humbly serve those who are in need or those who will not be able to return the service. Planning with your guests in mind will help keep your eyes on our humble Lord Jesus.

PERSONALITY IN PRACTICE

According to Abraham Maslow's hierarchy of needs, [1] people cannot safely experience joy without first having their basic needs met. Use

Maslow's pyramid to fill in ways that you will address your guests' most basic needs (and then preferences) in order to enable them to pursue greater fulfillment at your wedding. [11]

The categories for each tier of Maslow's hierarchy are written to the right of the pyramid. You can fill in each level of the pyramid with ideas that you can execute at your wedding to echo the essence of the hierarchy. For example, for Physiological, you might think about how you can keep your guests from being too hungry, too thirsty, too tired, too hot/cold, etc.

For Safety, you might consider how to lessen the financial burden on your guests or consider how Christian tradition might feel to non-Christian guests.

For Love/Belonging, you can consider aspects such as how the guests will be seated, which family and friends are invited and which aren't, how your bridal party will be announced, or how you will be able to connect with your guests.

For Esteem, how will you communicate your gratitude, how will you honor your parents, what will you write in your vows, or would you want a slide-show to demonstrate how well you have grown up?

For Self-Actualization, how will you challenge your guests to engage with Christ's purpose for marriage, what opportunities will you offer for your guests to be spontaneous in their enjoyment, are you praying for each of your guests, and what creative touches can you add to make the event above and beyond?

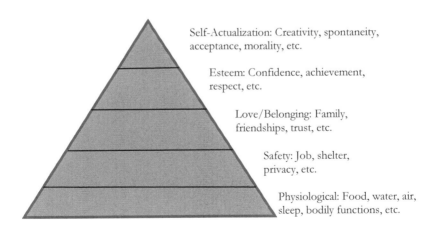

Self-Actualization: Creativity, spontaneity, acceptance, morality, etc.

Esteem: Confidence, achievement, respect, etc.

Love/Belonging: Family, friendships, trust, etc.

Safety: Job, shelter, privacy, etc.

Physiological: Food, water, air, sleep, bodily functions, etc.

PRAYER

Lord, You are the great provider who anticipates all of our needs. Show me what my guests will need in order to fully enjoy the wedding. Help me to plan with them in mind for Your sake. In Jesus' name, Amen.

PROBLEM PICTURE

"When the final list of guests was made we still needed to cut back. We decided to include a note to our single friends asking them not to invite a 'plus one.' This was a difficult decision as most of our friends were single and were expecting to invite a date, but it reduced our list by about 50 extra people. This was significant because my guest list worked its way into many details like what foods they would like, what music they would enjoy, what favors they would want, and—of course—which seats they would prefer. It was all tricky, especially having started with a guest list that was too big. Although I enjoyed the challenge of serving my guests, looking back, my favorite moment of the wedding was when Bob and I hid in a room after being announced husband and wife at the ceremony, waiting to make a grand exit to the reception site. We had about 15 minutes alone in that room, and it was great to be focusing on no one but each other. That moment was my gift from God at our wedding, a moment I didn't plan and a moment without the guests, reminding me what was important about that day."

-Joy Boyan

[1] *Maslow, A. H. (1943). A Theory of Human Motivation.* Psychological Review, *50*, 370-96.
[II] *For more information on Maslow's hierarchy of needs, see* http://www.simplypsychology.org/maslow.html

YOUR VENDORS

"Some give freely, yet grow all the richer; others withhold what is due, and only suffer want. A generous person will be enriched, and one who gives water will get water" (Proverbs 11:24-25).

PRINCIPLE: Look for ways to honor your vendors beyond integrity in your transactions, so they might see through you the extravagance of God's grace for them.

Your relationship with your vendors is unique. On the one hand, you are paying for a service or product at a price that meets the expectations of your agreement. It is a transaction.

On the other hand, your vendors are people whom you are inviting to one of the most intimate days of your life. You are trusting them and are sharing your life with them. This is a similar dynamic to that of a close friend except that it's (usually) one-sided and finite.

The intimacy that is forced by this **business transaction** is an invitation to share the love of Christ. If these people are paid to know what you will like for your wedding, why not share with them that you are a woman for the Lord. What pleases you is what pleases Him.

The ways in which you interact with the vendors will show your love for Christ. In other words, your vendors will experience Christ as they work with you. How awesome is that!

Another realization to keep at the forefront is that your vendors are people. Though your business relationship means that you don't have to settle for less than **excellence** in your transactions, you should be mindful of blessing the person behind the business.

In general, that means offering **grace**, showing **gratitude**, and working with **integrity**. Specifically, that might mean that you show up on time for appointments but offer grace if they can't. It might mean coming prepared with your ideas and listening to their feedback. Or perhaps offering them traditional gratuity, serving them a meal at your wedding, and writing a testimonial of their services. If the vendor is sub-par, then perhaps that will mean you graciously dismiss them from their duties and explain to them how they fell short so they can learn from their errors.

The vendors who are present at your wedding—musicians, photographers, and videographers—will get to hear your vows, the prayers, your toasts, and every other personal detail that gives glory to Christ. They are coming into the church service of your wedding without even knowing that they might encounter Christ for the very first time.

ADVICE FOR BLESSINGS ON YOUR VENDORS

-**Pray for each vendor by name.**

-**Communicate readily with your vendors, and capture your agreements in writing.**

-**Think about how you can bless them as they are blessing you.**

-**Come prepared.**

PERSONALITY IN PRACTICE

Have you ever done a random act of kindness? They are delightful because they are unexpected (and often anonymous). You never know how that one small act might reach someone on a particularly despairing day.

Your vendors are already receiving your check and your testimonial because of your business transaction. Can you think of other ways—unexpected ways—that you can surprise them with blessings?

Maybe you can bring them a snack when you meet with them; you can extend a wedding invitation to their spouse; you can write a mid-planning thank you note; or you can take their business cards to give to friends.

The opportunities are endless. Think of something that you could do for a vendor using the following resources:

1.   Your time
2.   Your money
3.   Food
4.   Your artistic creations
5.   Your relationships

6. Gifts
7. Stationery
8. Your wedding events
9. Books
10. Your attitude

PRAYER

Lord, You have blessed me more than I deserve. I know that I don't have to do anything for my vendors beyond meeting the agreements outlined in our contracts, but if I did, I know it would bless them. What can I do to show them Your extravagant and gracious love as I let them into this special occasion? In Jesus' name, Amen.

PERFECT PICTURE

"During my first meeting with my florist, I was reminded that my words and actions were continually being evaluated by everyone who was part of this elaborate and overwhelming process. 'I really like stargazer lilies—and I'd like the flower girls to carry replicas of the mother's bouquets... But otherwise, I trust your professional judgment and am sure you will come up with something lovely.' She seemed stunned and replied, 'So many women come in here with a million requests—all they want to do is throw a party. I can tell you aren't like that, and that's wonderful.' I remember a warm feeling that in my simplicity and trust, I had somehow shown this woman that a strong marriage was my priority."

-Christina Davis

PAIRED

*"Then the man said, 'This at last is bone of my bones and flesh of my flesh'; [...]
Therefore a man leaves his father and his mother and clings to his wife, and they
become one flesh" (Genesis 2:23-24).*

Helpmate. Partner. Lover. Friend. Confidant. Teammate.
Encourager. Spouse. Other-half. Greatest fan. Accountability partner.
Teacher. Leader. Servant. Exhorter. Soul-mate. Advocate. Protector.

When you say, "I do," you become one flesh with your husband.
Your life moves towards oneness in order to be a team for Christ. Marriage
is a spectacular and mysterious gift from the Lord, and now it's yours to
receive and cherish.

REGISTRY

"...they broke bread at home and ate their food with glad and generous hearts, praising God and having the goodwill of all the people" (Acts 2:46b-47a).

PRINCIPLE: As you and your fiancé build your home together, consider how you might use it as a place of worship and ministry.

You and your fiancé are **building a home together**—one where you can have intimacy with each other and fellowship with others. Your home will be a sort of church that takes in the needy, hosts celebrations, and teaches and worships with those who will join you. Your love for one another will be apparent in your home, and when guests visit you, they will see Christ's love through you.

How do you want your home to feel? If it's your refuge, it might feel cozy; if it's your sanctuary, it might feel austere. If it's your staging-ground, you might keep it simple and spacious; if it's your playground, you might make it exciting and comfortable.

You and your fiancé get to create your home together. The one you build now is likely to change with the seasons of your life, so you can bask in the freedom to build it for who you are now. If you later discover that it's not helping you to become the woman you want to be, you can always make changes.

Having a registry is one of the most beautiful ways to build your home. It's an opportunity for you to **practice receiving**, just as it is an opportunity for your friends and family to give generously to your marriage.

Vacuuming becomes so much more fun when you think of your friend who gave you the vacuum as your wedding gift. No matter how banal the item might be, when it's given in love, it can really be a treasure. Your home will be a tapestry of items that were chosen with care by people who love you.

Registries are also wonderful because they afford you opportunities that you might not otherwise have. Of course, you need to accept this privilege with humility, but you have permission to **dream a little**. Would you ever buy yourself a tent, a china tea set, or crystal candle sticks? Those are my items that I would have loved to have but would never have budgeted for myself. Whatever your items are, it never hurts to put them on the registry, especially if your receiving them will amount to great blessing for the guests or family members whom you will have in your home.

For you brides who rejoice in simplicity and truly do not want to accumulate "stuff" that you don't need, you can still give the opportunity to your friends and family to help build your home. There are websites out there that allow you to put a **fund** on the registry. People contribute amounts to whatever item/event you specify. For most brides and grooms, that ends up being a honeymoon—maybe a house or a car—but it can instead be for your first mission trip together or for any other grand cause that you choose.

ADVICE FOR REGISTRY BLESSINGS

-**Pray over your items and the rooms in your home.**

-**Choose a variety of prices for your registry items so that low-income and high-income guests alike can all find something they can afford.**

-**Have your registry ready to go before your first bridal shower invitations are sent. Be sure to update your registry closer to your wedding if most items are already purchased.**

Similarly, you can request that your guests **donate to an organization** that is dear to you and your fiancé. Even if their gift does not equate to an item in your home, it does contribute to the spiritual "home" that you two are building together.

However you see fit to create your registry, I recommend that you make one, if not for yourself, then for your guests. People want to give you something as a token of their support, and they appreciate knowing that what they are giving is something that you will cherish.

PERSONALITY IN PRACTICE

Putting words aside can really spark your imagination. In the house below, spend some time drawing the rooms of your home as you dream they will be, and have your fiancé do the same on a separate copy. This simple exercise can be very powerful for those who are more visual than verbal.

Share your drawings together as a conversation starter for how you can begin building your home and giving it purpose even now. Don't be surprised if differences in expectations pop up. Embrace them as an opportunity to learn more about each other for the sake of oneness in your marriage.

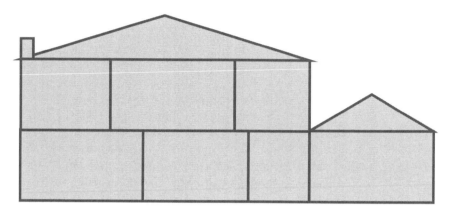

PRAYER

Lord, the roof over my head is a blessing that I never want to take for granted. Help us to make a home together that will bless Your kingdom in return. In Jesus' name, Amen.

PROBLEM PICTURE

"Jay and I married the fall after we graduated college. We were both 22. Our youthful vigor inspired some wonderfully courageous behavior like moving across the country to Los Angeles, but it really did not do us any favors in terms of registering for wedding gifts. Since we were both the oldest children in our families and the first of all our friends to get married, we really didn't have anyone else's current expertise and experience to depend on when registering and— most importantly— when deciding whether to return or keep certain wedding gifts. In that young, short-sighted fashion, we concluded that since we were currently on the pre-wedding 'South Beach Diet,' we would likely never again eat carbs, so of course, there would NEVER be a need for the fabulous and expensive KitchenAid mixer given to us by a dear family friend. In fact, wouldn't it be better to just cash in all of these 'superfluous' kitchen items and use the store credit to buy all our family and friends Christmas presents like gourmet olive oils, lemony dish soaps, and striped kitchen towels?! Although we do kind of regret not investing that store credit in a more practical set of cookware or the like, our hearts were actually in the right place. Especially when you marry young, it takes a couple of years to figure out what you want your home to look like and what activities around your home you want to focus on. It's really hard to speculate on those specifics when you are 22. The very act of getting married and maturing in that process changes what you desire in marriage. I almost died from a massive brain stem stroke when I was 26. I did not eat by mouth for almost a year after that. Since then, celebrating life, breaking bread, and being home have taken on much deeper, more sacred meanings. Nowadays, we love to entertain and cook and even eat carbs! In some ways, I wish we had kept that KitchenAid mixer years ago (oh, the years of homemade baked treats we missed out on!), but when my mother-in-law gave me one for Christmas recently, I actually appreciated it all the more because I could understand its value and see the specific role it could play in the story of my home life. In truth, forgoing some of the excess stuff early in our marriage in favor of loving each other well was the greatest gift to experience."

-Katherine Wolf

PRE-MARITAL COUNSELING

"Fools think their own way is right, but the wise listen to advice"
(Proverbs 12:15).

PRINCIPLE: You won't fully understand why you need pre-marital counseling until after you have been married, so go on faith knowing that the investment will pay out significantly in the future.

Deciding to marry someone can create a false sense of knowledge about that person, the assumption being that if you did not know your fiancé thoroughly, you would not have agreed to be his wife for the rest of your life. And if you know your fiancé completely, why would you ever need to have pre-marital counseling?

Married people will consistently tell you that a person doesn't know that he or she needs pre-marital counseling until after he or she is married. Though this reason can feel trite, it offers two pivotal truths: 1) Going to counseling is often **a matter of faith**, and 2) You can't know what marriage to your fiancé is like until you are actually married.

Counseling as a matter of faith is simply the concept that you are surrendering all that you know in hopes that you will learn more. It is **a matter of humility** that, regardless of how much you think you have already figured out, you are willing to be guided by experts for the sake of going even deeper in your marriage.

It also takes faith to seek counsel, because the nature of what you are being asked to reflect on drudges up pain. No one wants to deal with stings of the past, but if you believe that God heals, the **journey of reflection, examination, and repentance** becomes valuable.

Why are you the way you are? Why don't you change? Why can't you stand X, Y, or Z about your fiancé? Why do you practice a double standard? Why are you defensive about broaching topic X? Why do you lack confidence in Y area? Why do you practice A concept of money and B concept of domestic roles? Why do you have fear? Have you been wounded? Why does X irritate you? What do you love about your fiancé? Why did you choose him? How many children do you want? What if you can't have children? What holiday traditions are you going to foster? Which family traditions will you continue to embrace? Why?

Your pre-marital counselor will hopefully be more sensitive and organized than that list of questions, but he or she will pay attention to areas of your life that are trapped by pain, pride, or fear. He or she will prod those areas in hopes that you will let God in to restore you.

In terms of not knowing marriage until you are married, the basic principle is that what you currently know about one another doesn't directly correlate with *how* you will **become one flesh**. Becoming one flesh is a mystery that is only revealed as it happens. As much as you *know* each other, you still don't know each other in the context of marriage.

> ### ADVICE FOR PRE-MARITAL COUNSELING BLESSINGS
>
> -Choose a counselor with whom you are both comfortable sharing.
>
> -If sessions become heated, refrain from rehashing the information outside of the session. Wait until your next meeting, so your counselor can help you process well.
>
> -Pray, pray, pray.
>
> -Journal the truths that emerge and the resolutions that you make, so you can look back at the merciful hand of God.

The distinction of marriage from engagement is a blend of the new dynamic of shared schedules, finances, and dreams; the new level of intimacy and romance; the newfound priorities, fears, and hopes; and the new encounters with the Holy Spirit that come with the mystery of being one flesh. Marriage is simply different from pre-marriage. No matter how little you think you need counseling, trust in the advice of couples who have been down this road before you; you will gain tools and knowledge that you won't know you will need until you are positioned to use them.

As for what to expect, pre-marital counseling will often be done with the pastor who will officiate your wedding. Part of your time together will be to brainstorm and **finalize the ceremony details**. The bulk of your time, however, will be spent in exercises to cultivate good communication, to acknowledge expectations, to examine areas of hurt or hardness, and to cast a vision for oneness.

A good pre-marital counselor will have a keen ear and a sense of your emotional limits. He or she will help you untangle your reflections and will help translate those to your fiancé and vice-versa. He or she will **devise a tool belt** based on your particular needs and will give you exercises to take home and bring back to the next sessions.

At the end of each session, you might feel agitated or wounded because of the emotional toxins that are released through the counseling. You might feel hopeless because your time was up before a mutual resolution was reached between you and your fiancé. Take heart! With refining comes pain. But pain that emerges from **soul-work** will clear out junk and allow for more grace, healing, and redemption from the Lord Jesus.

For most couples, the number of sessions you have will seem too few, because your eyes will be opened to this new dimension of the unknown that puts all things known under a new scrutiny. But you will be more equipped than you will probably realize. Marriage will give you ample opportunities to put your tool belt into practice. If you still feel ill-equipped, go back for a tune-up session every now and again, or seek out a marriage counselor whom you can see regularly.

Seeking wisdom is a beautiful act of humility that can deeply bless your marriage. Be courageous and proactive (to the best of your ability) in asking for help.

PERSONALITY IN PRACTICE

Rather than asking probing questions that would be better answered within the safety of pre-marital counseling, I am posing questions about your concept of pre-marital counseling. Answer them individually and then have a conversation with your fiancé to find where you share beliefs and where you differ.

Consider sharing with your counselor the perspectives you each bring to the sessions.

1. When I think of counseling, I think of _____.

2. Some aspects of my fiancé's life that I know thoroughly are

_____.

3. Some aspects of his life that I want to learn more about are

_____.

4. My concerns about sharing in front of my fiancé are
   _____.

5. My concerns about sharing in front of a counselor are
   _____.

6. The style in which my fiancé and I communicate is
   _____.

7. The people who have modeled or taught me what marriage should look like are _____.

8. If someone found out I was going to counseling, I would respond by saying, _____.

9. The aspects of marriage that I anticipate being most difficult are
   _____.

10. The aspects of marriage that I anticipate being most seamless are
   _____.

PRAYER

Lord, I confess that I act as if I know more than You. Please guide my fiancé and me in becoming one. Only You truly know what tools we will need and who is best to teach them to us. Please give us humility so that we can be restored. In Jesus' name, Amen.

PERFECT PICTURE

"My husband and I are forever grateful to our pastors for teaching us about the importance of communication in marriage. The best tool we learned was 'The Three Things.' Each week we sit together and share about the week prior.

A Bummer—Something the other person did. The rule is: one person talks, the other person listens. The listener does not defend, justify or argue. I have shared things like how he hurt my feelings by being passive-aggressive rather than being direct.

A Solid—Something that the other person did that was solid, or really good. I have shared things like how I love that he always does the dishes after dinner.

A Home Run—The thing that the other person did that knocked your socks off. I have shared how awesome it is that he really listened to me that week and how I felt so loved and supported.

Nothing bad ever sits more than a week. We make a point to never miss 'The Three Things.' I love it because it lets me know what I'm doing that is working so I can do more of it and what isn't so I can watch it in the future."

-Andee Flynn

WEDDING NIGHT

"The human mind plans the way, but the Lord directs the steps"
(Proverbs 16:9).

PRINCIPLE: Communicate your wedding-night hopes and fears to one another, so no one suffers the defeat of unmet expectations.

This is it! The big night you have been waiting for. The magical, fairytale romance where you come together as husband and wife in the marriage bed.

Whether you have waited your whole life for this moment or whether you have come into a restored, new season of waiting, this night means something. You have an expectation for how it will go…and so does he.

The number one opponent you have to a successful wedding night is unmet expectations. One of the best things you can do is to **prayerfully communicate your expectations** for how your romance will play out— not that you have to stick to a script but that you are intentional about attending to the needs of your hearts, minds, spirits, and bodies. Because your needs will be different yet equally significant, you would be wise to do your due diligence before the momentous evening is upon you.

A simple way to understand and articulate your expectations is to consider the four main components that comprise you to discover any latent hopes and hindrances:

1)   **Heart.** Your heart, for this conversation, encompasses your emotions, including your hopes and your fears. You might very well have been told your whole life that sex is bad. If so, how you feel about sex now is probably jaded by the negativity you had associated with it in order to keep pure before. Your wedding night might be one of terror rather than ecstasy.

In addition to the potential fear of facing a life-long "enemy" this evening, you might have performance anxiety. You might be totally in the dark about the biology of sex, not to mention the techniques, styles, moves, and moods. Doing some research (within a close time frame to your wedding) can help to alleviate some of these fears.

Even the good emotions might creep up to hinder your experience. If you have remained pure in hopes of the perfect married sex life, you might be so hopeful for the evening that you don't have a mental slot to process the gritty logistics of sex. Or if you have had sexual abuse in your past, your expectations for joyful sex might not come to fruition as you had expected, especially if your past trauma is not already processed and healed.

If you have never experienced sexual contact before, because you have faithfully guarded your virginity and cherished the virtue of modesty, then you might be overcome by the feeling of embarrassment. Even though your vision of sex in marriage is pure, the act of doing it might not feel pure, because you are experiencing such vulnerability that you might feel overcome with panic, shame, or fear of being rejected.

On the other hand, if you have fallen to sexual impurity or if you have been sexually victimized, you might have deep shame that creates a defense mechanism. Being vulnerable on this night might stir up some guilt or some anger over previous sexual experiences that seem to violate the sanctity of this night.

2)   **Mind.** Your parents, your friends, your church, and your society all do their best to teach you their version of what sex is all about. Hopefully the teaching you have received and processed is in line with the Truth of the Lord. Rarely, however, is anyone free from a conflicting voice of influence.

So with everything learned, there comes a moment when that teaching is put into practice. It is tested and either confirmed, rejected, or adapted. Along with every experience comes a relearning of the truth you had previously acted on.

You might very well have ingrained misguided truth—or even flat-out lies—into your framework for sex.

How do you think God views sex? How did your parents view sex? How did you learn about sex? How have you tested your knowledge, and what conclusion did you come to? Is it going to be worth waiting for? Can you have redeemed sex if you have already had it outside of marriage? Are you worth waiting for? Can you be fully loved by your husband even if he didn't wait for you? What makes you beautiful? What aspects of passion are holy?

So many questions that God has answers for. Sometimes learning His answers means totally debunking the "truth" you were operating by. Not only does it mean admitting you were wrong and desiring to change your ways, but also it means dealing with scars from your years of misguided decision-making. All that to say, simply waltzing into the hotel room on the wedding night without having dealt with these misconceptions can darken and damper—and even wound—your sexual experience with your husband. That would then leave you with yet another misguided experience to confirm your false framework.

> **ADVICE FOR WEDDING NIGHT BLESSINGS**
>
> -Be well holistically. Get in shape, nurture your spirit, protect your heart, and focus your mind on what is pure.
>
> -Have fun figuring out how to please, adore, and cherish your husband rather than focusing on what you need him to do for you.
>
> -Practice boundaries for purity during your engagement.
>
> -Ask for counsel from trusted believers.

If your husband has sexual sin in his past, including pornography, you might also be battling the temptation to compare yourself to his past partners, real or in the media. You might flail at the idea that you are set apart above all others. Your mind is a battlefield for the enemy, and he will plant seeds of lies in your mind to distract you with terrifying thoughts.

Even if both of you have been pure, you might struggle with body image or spontaneity. You might be under the weight of the lies that you are not beautiful enough, you are not creative enough, you are not exotic enough...

Your mind needs to be taken captive by Christ (2 Corinthians 10:5). Those who have the mind of the Spirit have peace, which leads to life (Romans 8:6). Your faith is more precious to God than gold (1 Peter 1:7); you are the apple of God's eye (Zechariah 2:8), His crown and His delight (Isaiah 62:4-5). Your marriage is fused by the power of God (Mark 10:9). Your repentant heart has been received (Luke 15: 10) and restored by the blood of Christ (Romans 8:10-11). Passion in marriage is good (Song of Solomon 8:6-7).

Your mind needs Truth to set it free. If your expectations

are based on lies, you will struggle to experience the fullness of your marriage bed.

3)   **Spirit.** God is love. Our efforts to love are only empowered by God's Spirit at work in us. The further we are out of God's presence, the more we close off room in our spirits for God's Holy Spirit to thrive.

The best sex lives are those that stem from healthy prayer lives, from time in worship, and from obedience to God's will. God created sex and He created marriage. The more you are in accordance with His Spirit, the more you can experience the fullness of His intentions for sex and marriage.

Because sex is most fruitful when it is out of the desire to serve and please the other, sex will be most joyful when each spouse is filled with the Spirit in order to selflessly serve the other. It is hard to seek the welfare of someone else when your eyes are on yourself. The best way to move your eyes off yourself and onto those whom you love is by companioning with the Spirit.

Sex is a matter of worship. It is certainly a physical pleasure, but it is also a spiritual fusion between you and your husband, and it is pleasing to God; therefore, it is also an act of worship that begs for your spirit to be vibrant and obedient to Christ.

Pray, cherish solitude, store up rest, worship, create, serve, commune. Nurture your spirit so that your love tank[1] is filled in order for you to pour it out for your husband's sake, and vice-versa.

4)   **Body.** How you feel physically will fuel your sexual desire or lack thereof. If you are stressed, tired, cold, over-fed, hot, aching, or any other number of physical distractions, your sex drive will be challenged.

Sex can be uncomfortable for variety of different reasons, so in the midst of experiencing emotional bliss, spiritual union, and physical pleasure, you might also be distracted by the chafing of his facial hair on your face, or the weight of his body that stunts your airflow, or your hair that gets stuck under someone's arm and pulls.

Being in your best physical shape can help to avoid some of those painful distractions. Additionally, knowing your physical limitations and planning around them can also stave off a number of unwanted issues.

So what does this mean for your wedding night? Consider questions like, what time of day would you be checking into your hotel room? Is that at a peak energy time or a depleted energy time? If you are sweaty from being on the dance floor or hungry from missing your chance to scarf down dinner, will you be able to enjoy physical intimacy? If your body sizes are hazardous to one another, have you considered positions that will work? The list of considerations goes on.

What's so great about romance is that it can start with any act at any time of the day. The cliché that a woman's foreplay starts when her husband does the dishes actually serves as a framework for how to consider your physical limitations.

If stress is a mood killer, then consider taking your limo ride to breathe, to hold hands, to share your favorite moment of the day, to kiss, to show a little skin, to pray, and even to savor some silence. Use it as a break from the stress of the day and a reboot for the evening.

If sweat grosses you out, then check into your hotel room and take a shower together. Use that functional act as a way to flirt and entice.

If hunger and fatigue are sexual opponents, then have a meal. Break bread together, sip some coffee together, and savor the sweetness of dessert. Order foods that are aphrodisiacs or are conducive to intimacy (maybe lay off the onions and garlic). Your survival needs will be met while you are building up intimacy with each other.

If sex is wrapped up in fear or shame for you, take time to pray together before you do it. Be in worship together. Thank God for creating every inch of your body, thank Him for sex, and thank Him for giving you the love of your life. Petition Him to bless your evening and to cultivate a holy, passionate, undefiled sex life in your marriage.

If you and your fiancé can pray through these four components and determine your areas of need or concern, as well as your desires and hopes, you can **create a plan together** that will guide you through the evening.

Again, the plan is not rigid. It's merely a guide or perhaps even a Plan B if the organic, spontaneous Plan A doesn't seem to be as great as anticipated. The plan is also an intentional mode for letting both voices be heard.

There is a lot of pressure for the wedding night to be perfect. You two can release one another from that pressure by addressing your fears ahead of time (not too far out from the wedding date lest you arouse unquenchable temptation). You might even have the conversation of whether you have the permission from the other to let the wedding night happen the next night if either of you simply cannot make love that evening because of fatigue or any other severe hindrance.

No matter what happens that evening, you are still married. You have the rest of your lives to lie in each other's arms and figure out how to be one sexually.

PERSONALITY IN PRACTICE

Answer the following questions individually and prayerfully. With the exception of question three, do not share them with your fiancé until the week before the wedding (in order to limit temptation) or at your most discerning window of time. Question three should be addressed before your engagement (or early on in the engagement), if possible, and should be shared with honesty, but with limited details.

1. Whose model/teaching of sex have you learned the most from theoretically? Practically?
2. What Scripture have you used to confirm or deny what you have already learned regarding sex and regarding your sexual identity?
3. Do you have sexual sin you need to confess?
4. What emotional blocks keep you from a holy view of sex? From a desire for sex?
5. What lies about sex, about God, about your body, about marriage, or about your fiancé keep you from having peace about an unabashed and fulfilled sex life in your marriage?
6. Do you have any difficulty seeing the physical act of sex as a spiritual act of worship? Do you have any idea why you do or do not have this difficulty?
7. What physical limitations do you have? On your wedding day, which of those might be involved, causing a potential distraction from the joy of your wedding night?
8. What books have you read on sex within a Christian marriage? On the biology of sex?
9. How is your spiritual life? Are you basking in God's presence so you are at your best for your fiancé?

10. What one expectation do you have for your wedding night that must happen in order for you to have a great wedding-night experience?

PRAYER

Lord, how utterly amazing that I get to make love with my husband soon! Guide us in becoming one flesh. Restore us where we are broken, correct us where we are in error, and unite us where we are divided. May our sex life be to Your glory. In Jesus' name, Amen.

PERFECT PICTURE

"We had talked about what we were both expecting on our wedding night, and together we created a plan. When we got to the hotel room, we ate dinner. Then we showered together to begin the foreplay (and also to clean up). Then we dressed in our wedding-night attire, prayed together, and undressed each other at our leisure. We were both sensitive to the other's needs, which made for a pressure-free wedding night."

-Anonymous

---

[1] The term "love tank" is borrowed from the following book
Chapman, Gary. The 5 Love Languages: The Secret to Love That Lasts. Chicago: Northfield Publishing, 2010

HONEYMOON

"Come, my beloved, let us go forth into the fields, and lodge in the village; let us go out early to the vineyards, and see whether the vines have budded, whether the grape blossoms have opened and the pomegranates are in bloom. There I will give you my love" (Song of Solomon 7:11-12).

PRINCIPLE: No matter when you take it or where you go, have a honeymoon so that you can enjoy the novelty of oneness before you become distracted by daily routine and responsibility.

There is nothing more exhilarating than unadulterated time with the person you love. Just as spiritual retreats are refreshing to the soul, vacations and dates are refreshing to the marriage.

Up to your wedding, chances are you and your fiancé have been working or going to school in addition to planning your wedding. There probably hasn't been much time for the two of you to just get away and **enjoy one another** without a to-do list running through your minds.

The honeymoon is the most wonderful wedding tradition because it addresses that desire to run away with one another, **leaving your responsibilities behind,** in order to fully enjoy one another day and night. For most people, very few other times in marriage will this fantasy actually be made a reality.

Starting your married relationship by getting away with one another is a precious gift. You get to bask in each other's presence. You get to explore one another's bodies. You get to travel to exotic places. You get to wake up when you want and sleep when you want. You get to call all the shots together with no daily routine limiting your options.

Dreaming together outside of the restrictions of your daily routines and responsibilities is a bountiful exercise for a married couple. That's when the deepest desires of your heart come out and when you learn how to cast a vision together. That's when creativity flourishes and even when the purpose of your lives is explored.

To have space and time that is not beckoning you into the rut of routine, the burden of responsibilities, the comfort of the known, and the connections that are established allows you to be caught up in wonder, in sensation, in philosophy, in intimacy, in privacy, in spontaneity, and in all other things that are challenged by the practical nature of day-to-day life.

Additionally, on a honeymoon you get **time to rest**. You get time to come together with the Lord. You get time to indulge in His beauty. You get time to process and absorb the whirlwind of your wedding day. You get time to transition into being a wife.

Whether you fill your honeymoon with sight-seeing or whether you keep the agenda open for snoozes on the beach and afternoon jaunts, you have a time that is solely meant for **knitting you and your husband together as one** before the Lord.

ADVICE FOR HONEYMOON BLESSINGS

-Pray for your city of destination.

-Even if you are keeping a loose itinerary, do your research in advance, so you can simply choose and enjoy once you are there.

-Book your trip in your maiden name if your honeymoon is directly after the wedding.

-Bring dollar bills so you can tip without hassle.

Of course when you come back from your honeymoon, there will probably be a sense of let down, but that is natural. Take heart because although you are coming back to your same circumstances, *you*—as individuals and as a couple—will be different. You are better as two than as one. The routine you keep will have new purpose. The burdens you bear will be carried with new strength. The connections you have established will have a new dynamic. The known will transition into a new context. Life is exciting, and you have a teammate to live it with you!

If you have flexibility in the timing of your honeymoon, you might even consider postponing it until after you have moved in together, unpacked your boxes, and found places for your wedding gifts, and until after your wedding debts have been paid and your honey-fund has been replenished.

For those whose jobs are too demanding or whose bank accounts are too strapped, you can still create the essence of a honeymoon from where you are. It takes much more discipline than when you are physically far away from your daily life, but it is doable and it is necessary. Build in evenings that are communication-device-free, where phone calls and emails have to wait until you are ready for them. Take day-trips on the weekend to cultivate experiences together in locations that are beyond either of your comfort zones. Set aside a room in the home to be a work-less place where the two of you can simply be together without talk of work or routine.

However you have your honeymoon, have one. Claim and savor the rare opportunity to pour abundantly into your marriage so that as you walk in life together, you are doing so as one team, as one flesh.

PERSONALITY IN PRACTICE

One of the simplest ways to engage with your fiancé in the Kingdom of God abroad (or local) is to hang a map of the world (or city) on your wall and mark it with places that you want to pray for. If your map is against a bulletin board, you can use red thumb tacks for missionaries you are praying for, green for current events, blue for places you have been, yellow for places you want to go, and so forth.

Cultivating a practice with your fiancé of casting vision for the world at large helps to open your expectations for how God might want to use you. And consistently engaging in the needs of the world helps keep your eyes off yourself and on Jesus, who is the only One powerful enough to meet all of those needs.

Using this prayer tool as a means to come together with the whole world in front of you can also help you figure out where you might want to go on your honeymoon (or trips together later in marriage). Whether local or international, seeing it visually, engaging with it spiritually, and anticipating it mutually can add unity and significance to the places you choose to get away together.

PRAYER

Lord, send us away together so that we might adore one another and marvel at Your wonder together. Knit us together as one flesh, so we might return home with renewed purpose, vigor, and perspective as a team for Your glory. In Jesus' name, Amen.

PROBLEM PICTURE

"Besides dreaming of the perfect wedding day, I had always imagined a perfectly romantic honeymoon. My husband and I had decided that because we were moving from Arizona to Oregon three days after our wedding and were planning to have guests staying with us one week after moving in, we would plan our honeymoon a few weeks after the wedding so that we could get settled and be able to thoroughly enjoy our honeymoon. Needless to say, we certainly jumped right into life after the wedding. I was working so hard to unpack and set up the house before our guests arrived, and Jonathan was working long hours every day. Our honeymoon could not have come at a better time; we were more than ready for a perfect romantic get-away. Unfortunately, that is not exactly how it turned out. We arrived in Cancun and were disappointed to see that the weather forecast had only gotten worse; a hurricane was supposed to hit while we were there. Because the hurricane was approaching, it rained five of the seven days we were there. We found ourselves holed up inside with no extra money for excursions, because they were very expensive. We were battling sadness and frustration, but looking back, we are thankful for how the Lord used that time to teach us more about each other. We were forced to work together to make the best out of the situation—to seek enjoyment in what could be considered a dull and boring time. We ended up enjoying our time together and returning to the 'real world' without a false sense of what life would be like. Seeing where we are now in our lives and our marriage nearly a year later, we are both thankful for the lessons the Lord taught us during our honeymoon."

-Kelly Alexander

FOREVER

"...and the two shall become one flesh. So they are no longer two, but one flesh. Therefore what God has joined together, let no one separate" (Mark 10:8-9).

PRINCIPLE: The days of your marriage are but a blip against eternity, so cherish your husband in every moment.

Forever seems like a really long time.

In the case of marriage, forever is intended to mean for the course of one's life. Even that seems like a long time to love one person unconditionally and set him apart from all others, to team with him in life-long dreams and daily endeavors, to mesh with him through the irritating and the edgy, to trust and forgive him consistently, to sacrifice daily for his needs...the list goes on.

Marriage is a great challenge, but it offers even greater reward. You are in life together for the highs and the lows, the good and the bad, the plenty and the want. All of those become catalysts for refinery, creating one **dynamic journey** together with changing seasons and constant adventures.

God's design for marriage was **for a lifetime**. Even the few "outs" that Scripture permits are Plan B, for God hates divorce (Malachi 2:16). For all troubles in marriage, God is your contingency plan. He is your deliverer, healer, and redeemer. Give Him room to demonstrate His mercy and power, even if that means separating from your spouse while the relationship is unsafe or toxic in order to work on reconciliation. With God, there is always room for redemption and reconciliation.

If this is not your first marriage, know that God is merciful to forgive and heal whatever has happened in the past and is strong enough and gracious enough to work in your current marriage for the present and the future.

It is important that you have a realistic understanding of God's design for marriage, because it is true no matter how poorly marriage is modeled in our culture. It is also important that you know the cost of marriage, but it is even more vital to live each day with the hope of

knowing God more fully (and all of the joy, peace, and wonder that comes from Him) because of your marriage.

God will use your **marriage as a mirror** to show each of you what needs some work. His intention is for your refining within the safety of marriage, and He will use your love for each other to motivate you to change for Him.

With this constant growth comes indescribable joy. You will grow wise together, you will endure together, you will share experiences together, you will dream together, you will plant seeds and harvest them together, and you will seek God together.

All things beautiful and exciting that you can think of are made better when you experience them in the vessel of a healthy marriage.

The good times will be the best moments of your life. The rough times will challenge you deeply, but they will be invitations to lean on the Lord in ways you would otherwise not need or choose to do.

ADVICE FOR FOREVER BLESSINGS

-Pray together daily.

-Date each other, even after you are married. Stay friends.

-Surround yourself with other Christian couples in your same life-stage and some in the stage ahead of you.

-Go to counseling before you need to.

Take a step back and look at life with an eternal perspective: Your life here is to glorify God; it is temporary, and all pales in comparison to your eternal life with the King of Kings. When you view each day with this eternal perspective, marriage becomes one of the greatest gifts you could possibly receive. Who wouldn't want each moment of her life to be one that makes her more in the image of Christ? And to have companionship in the process? And, knowing that your life could end at any moment, do you not also want to endure the hard times for the sake of pouring into your husband, helping him to look more like Christ?

Forever becomes an uncertain amount of time in the most beautiful way. Each moment is precious and unique. The moments you spend with each other are all that you have together. When you live like that, you begin to do marriage in full color with 360° surround sound. You are awakened to the deeper, greater calling of a husband and wife who live for the Lord.

PERSONALITY IN PRACTICE

If you knew you were going to die tomorrow, what would you say to or do for your fiancé today?

PRAYER

Lord, our lives are short and so precious. Thank You for each moment that You have blessed us with. Thank You for each other. Please, Lord, may we bring glory to You. In Jesus' name, Amen.

PERFECT PICTURE

"When we met, we knew God had meant us for a bigger purpose than just to love each other. We had this term 'power couple' stuck in our heads, so we've set out to be just that. Having a purpose for our partnership helps us to think past just the here-and-now—what 'I' want—and makes us think of the life and time we've been given together on this earth and what kind of mark we're going to make for God's glory. Because of that, there were no cold feet when saying 'I do.' Our first home was chosen because we knew it would be a great space for a small group. When we had the opportunity to help build a church plant in our community, we jumped in. We've supported each other's dreams and made sacrifices wherever needed in order to help the other shine. The choice to have kids was a no-brainer, and adoption is something we discuss often because God has put it on our hearts. We take our finances and tithing seriously and try to think of everything we have as what God has given to us. Our relationship is no different. We love each other and have a great passion that some days is dimmed by stress and screaming toddlers, but not once have we let our minds think there's an option to give it up and start over. This is our gift, our life together, our responsibility, our love story, and our forever."

-Anonymous

POSTLUDE

"Therefore, as God's chosen people, holy and dearly loved, clothe yourselves with compassion, kindness, humility, gentleness and patience.

Bear with each other and forgive whatever grievances you may have against one another. Forgive as the Lord forgave you.

And over all these virtues put on love, which binds them all together in perfect unity.

Let the peace of Christ rule in your hearts, since as members of one body you were called to peace. And be thankful.

Let the word of Christ dwell in you richly as you teach and admonish one another with all wisdom, and as you sing psalms, hymns and spiritual songs with gratitude in your hearts to God.

And whatever you do, whether in word or deed, do it all in the name of the Lord Jesus, giving thanks to God the Father through him" (Colossians 3:12-17).

APPENDIX

RESOURCES

For all circumstances in life, I recommend that you first visit the Lord and seek Scripture for His guidance. In addition to *The Holy Bible*, the following resources are packed with wisdom:

COMMUNICATION

Laffoon, Jay and Laura. He Said. She Said: Eight Powerful Phrases That Will Strengthen Your Marriage. Grand Rapids: Baker Books, 2010

Chapman, Gary. The 5 Love Languages: The Secret to Love That Lasts. Chicago: Northfield Publishing, 2010

ENGAGEMENT

Boehi, David, et al. Preparing for Marriage: The Complete Guide to Help You Discover God's Plan for a Lifetime of Love. Ventura: Gospel Light, 1997

Thomas, Gary. The Sacred Search: What If It Is Not about Who You Marry but Why?. Colorado Springs: David C Cook, 2013

FINANCES

Dayton, Howard. Your Money Counts: The Biblical Guide to Earning, Spending, Saving, Investing, Giving, and Getting Out of Debt. Carol Stream: Tyndale House Publishers, 2011

Ramsey, Dave. Financial Peace Revisited. New York: Viking Penguin, 2003

MARRIAGE (GENERAL)

Driscoll, Mark and Grace. Real Marriage: The Truth about Sex, Friendship & Life Together. Nashville: Thomas Nelson, 2012

Feldhahn, Shaunti. For Women Only: What You Need to Know about the

Inner Lives of Men. Atlanta: Multnomah Publishers, 2004

Feldhahn, Shaunti and Jeff. For Men Only: A Straightforward Guide to the Inner Lives of Women. Atlanta: Multnomah Publishers, 2006

Harley, Jr., Willard F. Fall in Love; Stay in Love. Grand Rapids: Fleming H. Revell, 2001

Keller, Timothy and Kathy. The Meaning of Marriage: Facing the Complexities of Commitment with the Wisdom of God. New York: Dutton, 2011

Larsen, Dale and Sandy. Couples of the Old Testament: 9 Studies for Individuals or Groups. Downers Grove: InterVarsity Press, 2004

Rainey, Dennis and Barbara. Building Up Your Spouse. Little Rock: FamilyLife Publishing, 2010

The Significant Marriage® conference. Various locations. www.thesignificantmarriage.com

Thomas, Gary. Sacred Marriage. Grand Rapids: Zondervan, 2000

Weekend to Remember Getaway® conference. Various locations. www.weekendtoremembergetaway.com

Yerkovich, Milan and Kay. How We Love: Discover Your Love Style, Enhance Your Marriage. Colorado Springs: Waterbrook Press, 2008

PERSONAL HEALING

Cloud, Dr. Henry and Dr. John Townsend. Boundaries: When to Say Yes, When to Say No To Take Control of Your Life. Grand Rapids: Zondervan, 1992

Holcomb, Justin S. and Lindsey A. Rid of My Disgrace: Hope and Healing for Victims of Sexual Assault. Wheaton: Crossway, 2011

McGee, Robert S. The Search for Significance. Nashville: Thomas Nelson, 2003

Schaumberg, Dr. Harry W. False Intimacy: Understanding the Struggle of

Sexual Addition. Colorado Springs: NavPress, 1997

SEX

Driscoll, Mark and Grace. Real Marriage: The Truth about Sex, Friendship & Life Together. Nashville: Thomas Nelson, 2012

Leman, Dr. Kevin. Sheet Music: Uncovering the Secrets of Sexual Intimacy in Marriage. Carol Stream: Tyndale House Publishers, 2003

Penner, Dr. Clifford L. and Joyce J. Getting Your Sex Life Off to a Great Start: A Guide for Engaged and Newlywed Couples. W Publishing Group, 1994

SPIRITUAL GROWTH

Foster, Richard J. Celebration of Discipline: The Path to Spiritual Growth. San Francisco: Harper Collins, 1998

Hybels, Bill. Too Busy Not to Pray. Downers Grove: InterVarsity Press, 2008

Lewis, C.S. Mere Christianity. San Francisco: Harper Collins, 1980

Made in the USA
San Bernardino, CA
28 February 2014